Hobson's Choice

A Story of Love, Alcohol and Capacity

Kay Francis

GW00499259

Hobson's Choice: A Story of Love, Alcohol and Capacity

Copyright ©BKP 2022

First published 2022
by Bryant and Kay Publishing
Fochabers, Scotland
First Edition
BKP110

All rights reserved.

ISBN 978-1-910102-18-3

Dedication

This book is dedicated especially to Amy who is responsible for saving the life of the character in this book, also to anyone struggling with alcohol addiction and those involved in their care or wellbeing.

The Mental Capacity Act Section 2(a)

For the purposes of this Act, a person lacks capacity in relation to a matter if at the material time he is unable to make a decision for himself in relation to the matter because of an impairment of, or a disturbance in the functioning of the mind or brain.

Contents

Preface

This could be a story of any man. The names referring to anyone living or dead have been changed for the sake of anonymity. The author's name is also a pseudonym. The motivation for the book is the strength of feeling I had for a fellow human, notwithstanding that he was my ex-husband of twenty years, who had fallen so far into an alcoholic abyss, as to be barely able to walk, comprehend his predicament, look after himself in any way at all and who my son and I found homeless and desolate on a park bench. If he wasn't alcoholic before, then he certainly was now.

It is hoped that this story will resonate with others faced with the same predicament and with those who care for people with this seriously debilitating condition, brought about apparently by the sufferer's own choice.

In the light of current knowledge, it is maybe time to revise the concept of 'lack of capacity' in relation to alcohol related brain damage (ARBD) as defined by the Mental Capacity Act of 2005, and also, to seek to reform the perception of alcoholism held by society in general.

Acknowledgements

I wish to extend my lifelong gratitude to my mother, Marjorie Kay, for her support for my projects, her valued input and without whose love for the English language I would never have come to write at all.

I am also extremely grateful to my wonderfully supportive husband, Jaime Bryant, without whose technical expertise and dedication to the satisfaction of my seemingly never-ending requests for help, I would not be able to commit my ideas to print and achieve publication.

Introduction

This book relates the story of the life of a particular middle-class man, from his early years, who somehow and at some point in his life, became dependent upon alcohol. He is not alone. The sobering statistics show that UK consumption of alcohol reflects a level of drinking which is detrimental to health and will no doubt, ultimately have an impact upon health, social and emergency services.

- *24% of adults in Scotland in 2018 exceeded the revised low-risk weekly drinking guideline for both men and women (MESAS, 2020)*

- *The equivalent to 19.1 units per adult per week were sold in 2019. (14 units is the advised limit) (MESAS, 2020)*

- *In England 40% of men and 20% of women aged between 55 and 64 were drinking at a level considered to cause increased risk to health in 2019.* (Stewart, C., 2021)

The first section of three chapters describes the life of the man, his growing up and married life and the circumstances which led to what was maybe the beginning of the serious decline in the physical and mental health of an alcoholic.

Section two explains the series of events which brought this catastrophic cycle of alcohol abuse to a halt, but which was subsequently and unfortunately allowed to repeat.

The third section seeks to explain the condition of alcoholism, what might have caused this particular man to go down this road and poses the question, 'How does a middle-class man with seemingly few problems, a lovely home, family and job end up in the desperate state of a homeless alcoholic?' It then details the role and purpose of the Mental Capacity Act (2005) and examines the juxtaposition of this and of the services designed to help individuals such as Marcus, the main character in this book. The impact of alcohol upon the brain is then investigated and the book concludes with a discussion on the plight of alcoholics, perceptions of alcoholism and suggestions for how we might better serve such individuals suffering from this unfortunate and debilitating condition.

The information herein is related from my own experience, from organisations which deal with alcohol related issues, via website searches and reference to scientific articles. The website and journal articles are referenced at the back of the book.

Section One

Chapter 1

The First Thirty Years

Marcus was born in Kew in 1952, in the London Borough of Richmond upon Thames and lived in lovely semi-detached house set in a tree-lined avenue. He was the second and much-loved child of hard-working parents. Inherited from their Irish father, Marcus' father and brother shared a boiler making business. During WWII, they provided boilers and welding services for the aircraft factories. Marcus' mother worked at Somerset House, the office of the Inland Revenue, in The Strand and said that she very much enjoyed her time there, despite the war. There was great camaraderie and of course a time of great celebration at the end of the war. Marcus' mother and father were able to be married just before the end of the war and moved into their first home. Sadly, their new home was bombed, but luckily they managed to rescue many of their possessions and they moved to Kew.

Marcus reported having had quite a privileged childhood. He attended a private preparatory school in Sheen; although he did not like the masters. I suspect it was a bit too strict for him. He wasn't very interested in the boiler business but used to accompany his uncle to exhibitions of the steam engines which transported the boilers and was allowed to ride on the engines; this he did enjoy.

Sadly, Marcus' father became ill which, I was told by his mother, was mainly due to the poor air quality in

London, but possibly also due to excessive alcohol consumption. He had a problem with his lungs. The family had decided to move to Devon for the good air. However, before they could complete the move, his father died, in 1963 at only forty-four years of age, leaving his mother a widower at only forty-two, with two children to look after and her own mother. For the sake of a fresh start, his mother continued with the move and moved her family into a flat overlooking the sea in a beautiful seaside town on the south coast. With money from the boiler business, she ultimately bought a wonderful, detached house in quarter of an acre of land close to the sea, which comfortably housed Marcus, his elder sister, his mother and his grandmother. Although there was money for the house there was not a sufficient regular income, so his mother worked long hours in a local gift shop to keep them all. Marcus' sister also worked as a teacher after leaving university and before she got married and left home.

At the age of eleven, Marcus moved to a comprehensive school in Devon, a substantial sea change from a small prep school in London. As quite a good lookalike for Billy Bunter, both in shape and academic background and with ginger locks, he was initially a source of amusement, the butt of jokes and an immediate target for the bullies. In his early days of secondary school, he had weighed twelve stones. A good and lifelong friend however, came to his rescue, as did his PE teacher with whom he also remained friends, and visited even when I knew him over twenty years later. He lost weight through all the sport he was able to partake in and became a popular character and highly respected rugby player.

Devon offered quite an idyllic and healthy lifestyle. He was well cared for and could spend much of his time outdoors in his garden, by the sea or playing sports. He was an excellent student and did well academically.

One of Marcus' senior schoolmasters was concerned that he did not have a male role model, living in a houseful of women. He believed that Marcus needed more male companionship. He encouraged his love of sport and rugby and recommended that he be sent on an 'outward bound' course, something he was to regale everyone with for the rest of his life! 'Outward Bound' is an outdoor education program of personal development for youths which encourages people to make the best of themselves. Activities are undertaken such as climbing, abseiling, canoeing, sailing, kayaking and orienteering. Participants also learn skills such as working together, travelling, navigation and cooking, as well as how to live with others. This had a huge and positive impact upon him and certainly provided a wide range of experiences which he would build on in later life.

Leaving school is a big turning point for anyone and Marcus was unsure what route to take. He loved sport and the camaraderie and all round feelgood factors it gave him. He particularly loved rugby and played not only for his local team but for his county. He enjoyed the physicality of it, the purpose, the discipline, the feeling of belonging, the making of lifelong friends and the obligatory social life after the game. He decided that he would like to share this with others and that becoming a PE teacher would be an ideal career for him. He was accepted onto a teaching course at the local community college. However, he found some of the closeness and bonding exercises encouraged by the lecturer a little too much and decided that it was not for him.

He then decided to go inter-railing with his friend across Europe and fell in love with Greece and Italy and in particular an Italian girl, for whom he later attributed his loss of hair; something to do with a headboard! He visited Istanbul but found it rather 'raw', but Greece he found beguiling. This journey I believe, inspired his lifelong love of travel. As with alcohol, it took him away from daily realities and offered alternate and exciting stimulation; it was something he enjoyed immensely.

On his return he could not decide what to do and he worked for a short time for his mother's friend in a gift shop. Eventually he decided he would like to study law and was accepted at Aston University in Birmingham. However, after a year in Birmingham he decided that this was not for him either. He found the studying too hard and serious. He needed something a little lighter.

Marcus' mother was bitterly disappointed at this second failure and rather annoyed. She welcomed him home of course, but exhorted him to keep looking for something else. Eventually he settled on taking a degree in history at Manchester. This was a success and there are many avenues which those with a history degree can follow. We once met a group of girls who met up annually on holiday, they had all studied history together. One was a teacher, one an archivist, one worked in a museum and another in administration.

As her children left home and her mother passed, a large house with a quarter of an acre of garden on a slope to mow was too much, so Marcus' mother moved to a flat. She had a spare room and a balcony from which she was able to see her old house and the sea. The balcony always appeared to have year-round good weather and she was always able to sit on it, sheltered from the wind but enjoying the sunshine. Apparently, on his eighteenth birthday Marcus sent his mother out and had a party. She returned home to be asked who she was by a stranger opening her door to her and then to see Marcus depositing the contents of his evening's revelries from the balcony. She sent everyone home and Marcus was made to clean up. Whether or not his journey to alcoholism had begun then, who knows? Many teenagers and students have alcohol infused birthdays and go on to tell the tale at a later date, yet learn to control their drinking habits.

Following the successful completion of his degree, Marcus then had to decide what to do with the degree. He took a post graduate qualification in librarianship in Richmond, London for a year and became a chartered librarian. This enabled him to secure work for life; plus his innate charm, his outgoing personality and his affective presence, which made everyone around him feel at ease.

He settled for a year or two with a lovely girlfriend and a position as a librarian on local government scales at Swindon College. After seeing a post advertised in the north of Scotland, he thought he would enjoy an all-paid round trip and a chance to see the scenery, but as luck would have it, he was offered the post of Tutor Librarian and decided to stay. This post fulfilled his initial desire for teaching as it was partially a teaching role. He would be required to take an additional teaching qualification and to teach students how to find information and relevant resources for their courses. He seemed to be on a promising career path. His relationship with his girlfriend unfortunately fizzled out, most likely due to the problems of maintaining a long-distance relationship.

Chapter 2

Early Adulthood

His second year as Tutor Librarian at the college was when I met him in 1982. He was thirty years old and had apparently hidden all his cards on his birthday so that no-one knew he was so old!

He was very charming, kind and generous. He got on well with everyone and had many friends. He was a member of every sports club and enjoyed a varied social life. When I arrived as a new lecturer to the college, I got my car accidentally locked in the car park and he found a caretaker to let me out. After this generous gesture we became friends and he offered to make me a meal at my house. I was duly impressed by his home-made prawn cocktail, sole bon femme (sole with grapes in a white wine sauce) and a home-made cheesecake for dessert. We started to go out a couple of times a week. Most days after work Marcus would shop for fresh ingredients for his meals and enjoyed cooking. He enjoyed sailing and was a member of the college badminton and squash clubs, the local gym, the local tennis club and of course the local rugby club, where he was the Chairman. He also went out with his friends drinking.

I didn't actually seem to see very much of Marcus. This quite suited me as I spent most of my time when I was not at work, preparing lectures. The time spent with him was good, we went for meals, socialised with his friends and went walking in the beautiful Scottish countryside and the beach. This all appeared to be very 'normal' but he never seemed to have any spare money. Most of it seemed to go on food and drink. In the second year of our relationship, I became concerned about the quantity and frequency of his alcoholic intake; he never appeared to be 'drunk', despite observing him consuming quite high quantities. I asked him if he drank every day. He said that he did but that so did everyone and what was the problem? I doubted that his friends with families went out drinking every night. At one point I asked him to consider that he might be drinking too much and that I thought that every day was excessive. He did not like such conversations which rendered him capricious. I questioned his ability to stop. To prove a point, he didn't drink for three days. I think those are the only three days in the last forty years where he has voluntarily not had a drink of alcohol.

Alcohol is very much part of Scottish culture and its consumption is a way of life. I am sure that there are many Scots who indulge daily and some who binge drink, so to some extent his behaviour was 'normal'. Despite this, I doubted that many men drank as regularly and as heavily as Marcus and somehow still managed to look like they hadn't been drinking. I also suspected that when many of the men got married and had families to keep, then they could not afford either financially, time-wise or morally to keep up the pace of the drinking of their earlier days. It was more usually reduced to one night per week.

Marcus was always polite and courteous; he was good natured and good humoured. He was very popular and most people would attest to his amicable jocundity. Who or why would anyone challenge him about something which did not appear to affect him or those around him adversely? This seemed like a reasonable argument. He was very fit and healthy. He ate well and did lots of exercise.

He lived in a shared house in the town; I presume he drank every night. When I first met him, he had his neck in a collar and was not able to play rugby as he'd had an injury caused from playing. He told me that once when the bus had called on a Sunday morning to take him to a match, he was too hung over from the night before and was still in bed. There had been a big furore about getting him up and out in time for the game, not least because he had all the team's shirts! It was the cause of great hilarity.

At one point he went to Jordanhill College to take the teaching qualification he had agreed to complete when he started the job. From what he reported, most of the time was spent socialising. He never actually completed the course but somehow received the certificate. Having gained the qualification, there was an expectation that he would begin planning courses and prepare to teach some students. He did not however, have any wish to teach; he saw other lecturers struggling with unruly students and the suggestion made him feel ill. He began to say that he was stressed at work, he thought that people were 'out to get him' and he really wanted to leave. He had been there three years.

Looking back, I think that alcohol caused him anxiety. It certainly made him paranoid. I was unaware of this at the time. He maybe used alcohol as temporary stress relief, but his excessive consumption no doubt also caused him to be depressive and anxious. Although he was very sociable and not anxious when I was with him, it seemed there was always a problem with the people at work.

I loved my life in the North of Scotland. I had a lovely home, a great job, good friends and an intelligent, kind and caring boyfriend who was great company. He applied for and got a post at a college in Yorkshire. I sold my property and we moved to rented accommodation in 'The Last of the Summer Wine' country. I also got a post in a local school; this was at the beginning of the academic year of 1984.

After a year in the Yorkshire college, Marcus said that he would have to leave. He was getting stressed. The people there got on his nerves. He told me that I couldn't possibly understand how it was and what he had to put up with. He started looking for another job.

I was starting to wonder where our relationship was going. During the next year we decided to get married and Marcus found a job in Berkshire. His interview was apparently held in a pub because he was on holiday at the allotted time and so the interview had to be held outside of working hours. This of course went well, as he was in an environment where he felt most relaxed and comfortable. After a beautiful wedding in a hotel overlooking the Yorkshire moors and a honeymoon in the Greek islands (by the way, he packed Imodium), we moved to Berkshire in 1986 to start our married life. I was lucky to also secure a post in a different college in Berkshire.

Even at the beginning of this job Marcus was paranoid about his staff knowing anything about him. Some of his staff brought wedding presents to the house when he wasn't there and I was grilled about what they might have seen in the house and what questions they asked. I found this odd but retrospectively realise that it was his drinking that he wished to hide. I am not aware that the house was full of empty bottles, so unless they opened cupboards to look for evidence, I don't know what they could possibly have seen.

The day-to-day life was happy. We went to work, went on holidays, went out for meals and had a good social life. No-one would think that there was a problem. Was there a problem? Marcus ate well as he was a great cook, he was always a member of a gym which he attended daily, he played squash and any other sports available where we lived. He was probably a little overweight but generally he was healthy. Nor was there a problem with Marcus' behaviour because of alcohol consumption, it didn't seem to affect him. He didn't become rowdy or aggressive. If anything, he became more laid-back and sociable. I would say he had a high functional tolerance to alcohol.

If I ever broached the subject of his daily drinking, which was most likely above any daily advised limits (I don't think these were advertised anywhere then) he pointed out that it didn't cause him any obvious problems. When we went out, I always drove. Probably a high percentage of our income went on alcohol. Our finances were always separate as we both always worked, so I have no idea how much money went on liquid refreshment.

After a couple of years, I got a post at the same college as Marcus which was much nearer for me and we could even walk to work. I found that whilst he was outwardly very sociable and appeared to like everyone at work, in the privacy of our home he complained about everyone at work. He also worried again that he might be required to teach; it was suggested that he run a course on Information Studies. His anxiety heightened; in addition to worry about having to teach, he was almost in a constant state of anxiety that anyone would know anything about him or speak about him. He was again quite paranoid.

Marcus' mother had recently had a heart attack and this made him worry about his own health and that he might suffer the same fate. One night he insisted that he was having a heart attack. I didn't think so and tried to argue my point, but as he more robustly argued and pointed out, I'm not a doctor. He persuaded me to call an ambulance. The paramedics were wonderful and said that maybe he had done too much exercise and eaten too much, which I am sure was the case as he had just returned from the gym and eaten his evening meal. They said that he probably had indigestion, which has similar symptoms to a heart attack. I was not allowed by Marcus to answer any questions, so I suspect that he did not mention any alcohol intake to the paramedics. I don't remember what his consumption that evening might have been, if in fact any; I never kept a record and as it was his 'norm' I pretty much ignored it as it didn't seem worth arguing about. I had tried many times with no positive outcome.

I suspected at the time that his alcoholism was causing him to panic as he was experiencing the symptoms of tachycardia (faster than normal heartbeat) and a pain in his arm; he also complained of feeling light-headed and nauseous. As you will read about further in this book, tachycardia is also a symptom of heavy drinking (or any alcoholic consumption if you possess a particular type of gene). Alcohol causes the blood vessels to dilate which makes it increasingly difficult for the heart to pump blood around the body. It therefore beats harder and faster in an attempt to pump the blood round as it should.

Alcohol is also a diuretic which causes the body to rid itself of water and salt. The effect of this can be dehydration and may have contributed to Marcus feeling light-headed. Alcohol is also a depressant and may well have induced his feelings of panic and imaginary impending danger. I am sure that his physical symptoms were real but that mentally he was over-reacting. The similarity with the symptoms of indigestion provided a convenient cover for the alcoholic consumption.

Marcus would not however, be placated by advice from the paramedics. A doctor followed within an hour and told him the same, he needed to take it easy, he had overeaten. There was no mention of alcohol. Marcus did not believe the medical professionals; he believed that he had had a heart attack and that he would likely die in his sleep. He demanded that I sit awake all night on a chair next to his bed to ensure he did not die. It is very difficult to argue with someone who is so adamant in their beliefs and genuinely in fear for their life. This was in the autumn of 1987; it was a red flag then, but no-one saw it waving.

He still stuck to his convictions in the morning and persuaded his doctor to conduct an ECG on him that week. The results of course showed that he had not suffered a heart attack.

After four years at the college in Berkshire, Marcus found a new post on the South Coast for the beginning of the academic year of 1990. This was a return to local government scales, no longer on the lecturer scale. He believed that this would ensure that he would not have to teach, so he thought this would be a good move.

As I was pregnant, I was not in a position to find a new job. We sold up and moved to Hampshire. The anxiety began almost on arrival in this post and he began an earnest search for something else immediately. He was there for less than a year.

Marcus enjoyed ballet and whilst living in Hampshire we went to see a Russian ballet in Portsmouth. As always, before leaving the house Marcus maybe worried that he wouldn't be able to have a drink (or enough) so he downed a pint of lager before we set off, telling me that it was perfectly fine to have one pint and drive. Two pints of beer was said to put someone over the legal limit of 80mg of alcohol per 100ml of blood. This was legislated in 1981. On arrival at the theatre there was time before the show for another beer and a third at the interval. He was now over the limit. On leaving the theatre our car was parked under a streetlight. We got in the car and set off for home, Marcus was driving. I wasn't driving as I was heavily pregnant. A police car followed and stopped us. Marcus politely asked what the problem was. The policeman said that he did not have his lights on. Marcus explained that parking under the streetlight had maybe tricked him into thinking his lights were on. The policeman was happy with this reasoning and bid us a good evening. I thought it was a lucky escape, as if he had been breathalysed, he would surely have lost his licence.

His next post was in Suffolk and he moved into rented accommodation. It took me an extra year to sell the house and move to Suffolk; the housing market was very depressed, house prices had plummeted, so I spent the first year on my own with my young son.

I moved to Suffolk in 1992 and it was a good one for me. It was a beautiful, rural area with a dry climate. We lived in a friendly cul-de-sac with other young families. I spent seven quite happy years there. This was not the case for Marcus. Marcus' mother moved to Suffolk too and lived nearby, but sadly in the autumn of 1993 she suffered another heart attack and this time did not recover; she was seventy-two years old.

On top of this, as with every other job, Marcus was not happy at work; he stuck nearly four years at this college. Nor was he happy in the UK. He decided that he would like to live in New Zealand. I felt that he was running away. In order to be accepted, he needed to get a medical. We both had to have a medical. Even if I didn't want to go to New Zealand, which I didn't, I had to go through the application process because I was more highly qualified than Marcus and he needed my points on his application. His age was also against him for points; I was eight years younger. We went together for the medical. Marcus was very stressed prior to this as he knew that the doctor would ask about his drinking habits. I was told that I must say that he only had two drinks a day.

Marcus got accepted for New Zealand in 1995 and decided to give it a try. My four-year-old young son and I took him to the railway station and waved goodbye. I stayed in Suffolk. Financially, for me it was a very difficult time; my son had started at a private school and

I was working to pay for that and cover the bills. Marcus was in New Zealand for around six months. He did not find a permanent job and was unsure if he wanted to move there or not. When he came back he decided that he might try a different line of work and got a post as a sales rep for a company that sold library furniture. The job was in London. I did not want to go to London and did not want to move at all. Marcus found digs and went to London. By fluke he drove past the cemetery where his father was buried and was able to visit it and renew the stones on his grave. He had maybe gone in a circle in his life. After a few months he decided that he did not like the work or life in London and asked if he could have a transfer. He moved to another familiar area — Swindon, where he had worked after completing his post graduate qualification and before moving to Scotland. He moved back in as a lodger with an old friend and his wife. In time, of course this job got him down too. They wanted too much of him. I suspect that he had rather too many nights out with his friend. Between Suffolk, New Zealand, London and Swindon two years passed.

Marcus then returned to Suffolk but with no job. There was a stipulated time of two years, after which his chance to live in New Zealand would expire if he did not return, so he decided to go to New Zealand again. When our second son was two weeks old he took a bus to London and said he might or might not go to New Zealand. Two weeks later he phoned to say he was sailing around Wellington harbour! This was maybe the final straw for me. My parents gave me money to live on. I couldn't work with a new baby, I couldn't get benefits as my husband had only just left and had he actually left me? After a few months I told him to stay if he liked it. I was prepared to get on with life on my own. He came back.

Again, he started a job search and eventually was offered a job in Oman in 1998. This was a big move. Maybe this was a chance to start again and it was a dry country. This would be a big challenge. I agreed to go. However, it took two years for the onboarding process to be finalised and in the meantime, Marcus took a job at a college in Yorkshire. I stayed in Suffolk until the house was sold and then in rented accommodation until the end of the school year so that my son could complete it. We were together in Yorkshire for a year before we moved to Oman in August 2000.

Prior to our departure for Oman, we bought a house in Scotland where we first met. Life seemed to be full of circles. We stayed in this house for a holiday in the summer of 2000. I stayed home with the children while my husband went out for the evening with an old friend who had been his best man. When they arrived back by taxi, my husband stumbled out of the car and tripped over the pavement falling headlong into the garden fence. With no hair for protection, he incurred two very deep lacerations to the top of his head. I decided that it would probably be impossible to stitch the thin skin on the top of his head, so there was little point in going to A and E. This and the fact that he was somewhat inebriated, prevented me from taking him there. I applied an ice pack to his head with instructions to hold it there and put him in a spare room. His friend left in a taxi but despite me having given the taxi driver instructions, neither of them could remember which exact house he lived at, so after driving up and down his street many times, the taxi driver gave up and dropped him at the local police station until he was able to remember his exact address in the early hours of the next day and be taken home. His wife was not too pleased.

I questioned myself often whether I should worry or not worry about Marcus' drinking. I clearly did worry, but there was nothing I could do about it. I was the only person who could see any detrimental effects and to challenge the status quo was a mood changer.

The storytelling of alcohol-related incidents which are often amusing when related after the event, is not unusual in Scotland. Maybe herein lies a problem, the fact that the stories are always considered amusing. It is almost like slapstick humour. People when drunk do things they would not do when sober. They become invincible or behave in outrageous ways. For much of the time, the imbibing of alcohol is synonymous with relaxation, enjoying time with friends, exchanging stories and falling into deep sleep at the end of it all. Whether the occasion was remembered or not, it was sure to have been a good one. Would it be the same if everyone went to a pub and drank soft drinks? The social landscape would be more subdued without raucous 'under the influence' youths and rambunctious revellers in a town.

I'll share with you another story of a rugby team friend of Marcus'. The man in question had a reputation of being a 'hard man' and able to knock back a few 'swallies' (Scottish for alcoholic beverages). On this particular occasion he was out for a swally with some friends, not an unusual event in Scotland. The night turned into day and eventually the man staggered home and up his garden path. He was horrified to see suitcases on the path and was in panic. His wife must have finally had enough and packed his bags! As he got to the door, it opened. His wife was fuming and shouting at him. He had completely forgotten that they were going on holiday. His wife and children were packed and awaiting the taxi to take them to the airport. With great relief, he had a quick wash and brush up and was able to go on holiday. This couple are still married but I am not aware of the current condition of the man. I can only assume that he may be in a similar one to that of my now ex-husband unless he was lucky enough to have had some help to stop drinking; I doubt it.

Heavy drinking is mostly considered to be a normal and acceptable part of Scottish life. The whisky industry is synonymous with Scottish identity and even primary-aged schoolchildren are taken on school trips to see the whisky making process.

The Scottish Health Survey in 2019 reported that 1 in 4 people drink at hazardous or harmful levels (more than 14 units per week) and the National Records of Scotland (2022) reported 1,245 alcohol-specific deaths in 2021 (with alcohol being the underlying cause of death).

My husband, soon after the fence headbutting escapade, had to start his new job in a 'dry' country with two large scabs running the length of his head which were impossible to conceal. He told anyone who asked that he had had a 'run-in' with a garden fork.

Chapter 3

The End of a Road

I t was exceedingly hot, humid and uncomfortable on arrival in Oman in August. I didn't want to stay. The accommodation had cockroaches; it was filthy. The hot water taps had cold water and the cold water taps had hot. There were no plugs in the bath or sinks. The whirly gig in the dry excuse for a garden had no lines. The boxed, air-conditioning units fitted into the walls did little to cool the air and the ceiling fans sounded like something from a helicopter take-off pad and it was impossible to sleep. I had no washing machine. My husband's job was through the British Council but at a college. A kind lady from the British Council took pity on me and took my washing to be done. It was returned washed, folded and ironed, even my pants in neat little triangles. Life did get sorted out and we got a lovely house to rent, I got a job at the British School which paid the school fees for both boys. Without this it would have been almost impossible to live on Marcus' salary. In contrast with people who worked there in the oil industry, education was not particularly well paid. The house rent and the school fees would have taken all the money.

I had half-hoped that there would be no access to alcohol, but this was not in fact the case. We each had a quota. I have no idea what my quota was as I never saw it. Marcus used up our allowance of alcohol. I suppose I had just got used to Marcus drinking and he always told me it was 'normal'. He drank every day. I used to wonder that if he was ever breathalysed in a morning would he fail a test? I don't know how he managed to function at work. He clearly did manage to function at work, but our neighbour and his boss also lived next door. He used to come to our house in an evening and obviously noticed that Marcus was drinking. His boss was Jordanian and Muslim and we were living in a Muslim country. He asked me if Marcus was alcoholic. I said that in honesty I didn't know. He drank every day, did this make him an alcoholic? I assume that dependency makes you an alcoholic. Well, he did go for three days without a drink, nearly twenty years previously. He told me that he was absolutely not dependent and that he could stop if he wanted, he just didn't want to. How could I ever have checked if that was true? I did believe that he didn't want to. The extent to which he would have been able, I do not know. I expect it would not have been easy, even then.

Our house was large with five bedrooms, so we had enough for one each and a spare for visitors. Intimacy was rare. We lived most of the time like two old friends. In honesty I didn't like the smell of Marcus. It reminded me of the rancid odour of the bus conductor on my school bus, it used to make us all feel ill. I remember it still. I realise now that the smell was of stale alcohol. It's quite repulsive.

For much of our married life we had not lived together, as Marcus often moved on to the next job before I could get one or we had to sell a house and I had to wait until it was sold before I caught up. He was a year in Suffolk while I was in Hampshire and he was in New Zealand, London, Swindon or Skipton for most of the time that I was in Suffolk. I suspect that he had drunk even more when he was away than he had at home.

In Oman there were several occasions where Marcus had drunk way beyond any normal or acceptable amount (I question now what is normal or acceptable). One time we visited some Scottish friends, renowned for their hospitality. Marcus only left when their house was completely dry; I was quite embarrassed. I also had a problem trying to get a taxi to agree to take us home, once they saw the condition that Marcus was in. It was certainly not legal to be drunk in a public area, whatever the time of day or night.

I was sent to the shop one time to get a fly swatter as flies bothered him unusually (I later found that this is a symptom of alcoholism). He couldn't go to the shop himself of course as it was necessary to drive. I came back with two. He was quite angry and asked why I didn't get ten! This made me laugh; I only went for one. His behaviour became more unreasonable and he was paranoid about many things. One time he told me that his office at work was being bugged and that he was being spied on. He worked in a college library, not MI6. I went to his office with him on a Saturday to check it out in an effort to reassure him that this was not the case. His computer had a virus and had thrown up a date that only by coincidence was my birthday. There was no-one spying on him. I wondered why he would think such a thing. Yet more paranoia. I was to later learn that this too is a symptom of alcoholism.

This was not a happy time. We didn't go out together anymore; we were more disconnected than ever. He was in fact, I decided, more in love with alcohol than me and his children. One day I emptied any bottles I could find down the sink. He told me I was being childish. He re-iterated that he only had a couple of drinks a day. There was an element of truth to this; he probably had two pints of lager, two gin and tonics, two glasses of red wine, two vodkas and a couple of whisky chasers.

The situation worsened and I decided to leave him. We had been together for twenty years. I had given it my best shot. I had a full-time job and found accommodation, but he wouldn't let me leave and threatened to take the boys from me if I left. I am sure this was an empty threat, but I wouldn't have chanced it. Our neighbour and his boss decided to send him away to a different college. He refused to go, so we packed up to return to the UK.

Section Two

Chapter 4

Return to the UK

U pon arrival at the airport, Marcus seized his bag and left. I was left standing with two young children aged ten and four and suitcases of summer clothes. It was January, 2002. I made my way to my mother's house. Marcus booked himself into a hotel and took out all the money from our joint account. I was able to stay in an empty house courtesy of my brother's girlfriend; the house was for sale and unfurnished, so it was only a stopgap. My brother lent me his car too, so I was able to get to and fro. My mother and brother gave me money to live on.

I managed to find a property to rent close to the school that my eldest son had attended previously, near Skipton, to maintain some sort of continuity. I found myself a solicitor and began divorce proceedings. I was advised that a female one might be more 'on my side'. It turned out that she was alcoholic, but I didn't know that at the time. She asked me if my husband drank in the mornings. I said that he did not. *"Then he is not alcoholic"*, she told me. I was rather upset at this reaction and phoned Alcoholics Anonymous for advice. I listed the examples of unreasonable behaviour, his anxieties at work, his many job changes, his phobia of flies, his paranoia and general day-to-day behaviour. The lady on the phone stopped me before I got half-way through my list. She told me that there was no doubt at all that his behaviour was that of an alcoholic and advised me to advise him to seek help. As he would never admit to being alcoholic and spent a lot of his time and energy in covering up the fact and refused to enter into any conversation about it, he was very unlikely to do this.

As the father of our children, he was obliged to provide maintenance. The Child Support Agency contacted him. He told them he couldn't afford to give me any money. He was working full time in a professional capacity at a college in Gloucester. The only money he sent was in the form of a one-off postal order which had to be paid into a bank account. It was made out to the boys. They didn't have bank accounts. He believed that I would take the money, he told them. What exactly he thought I would do with ten pounds, except buy food or pay bills I don't know. So, no money was forthcoming.

The divorce was quite quick; we were granted half each of everything, which was in fact nothing, except a mortgaged house in Scotland. Marcus paid the mortgage for a year then stopped. The house was due to be repossessed. In the school holidays in 2003 I went to Scotland and stayed in the house, looking for a job. I had a call from my solicitor saying that I had apparently abducted the children. I still don't know how you can abduct anyone from the UK to the UK, to their own home. It was a very stressful time. Eventually I found work, moved into the house and took on the mortgage. Marcus was very bitter that I had left. He contacted the boys' schools and tried to cause trouble. He sent me letters from his solicitor which I returned unopened.

He visited occasionally and on one such occasion told me that he had stopped drinking for three months. I made no comment as it was the only time that he had ever spoken a word of admission that he was addicted to alcohol. He told me however, that he couldn't keep it up.

Rather than have to send money to me and his children he took early retirement at age sixty and after living in Gloucester and a couple of unsuccessful attempts to settle in Scotland, moved back to Devon. He had two work pensions and received his state pension at the age of sixty-five. On the two occasions he moved to Scotland he was required to leave his accommodation due to alcohol-related incidents. My eldest son visited him one day in Scotland and came home very upset because of course, he was drunk and it was only lunchtime. I began to wonder if he was now drinking in the mornings and whether or not this would now qualify him as being alcoholic (according to my solicitor's definition). He ended up back in Devon.

I encouraged my sons to keep up contact with their father and to visit whenever possible. As the boys grew older, they were able to travel independently to visit him. These occasions were not always positive ones. I received reports one time that his wardrobe was full of stripy label Tesco lager. He was no longer driving; I assume that he had lost his licence. I believe that he hasn't driven since his time in Gloucester. Over the last ten years and until 2019 I did not hear much about him.

My sons visited him in Devon in May 2019 for a holiday and booked themselves into a hotel. Marcus visited them in their hotel (under the influence of alcohol) and whilst in their hotel room, he forgot where he was and undressed for bed. He then walked through to the hotel lobby in his underwear, as he thought he was in his own home; a humiliating experience for all. He was also unable to attend a lunchtime meal which was booked, due to being intoxicated and unable to leave his accommodation. What impact this had on my sons I can only imagine. I had as little as possible to do with him. Everyone assumed, of course, that he was choosing to get himself into this state, where he would then engage in such unacceptable behaviour. The hotel staff, other visitors, my sons, myself and police, when they were called, blamed his unwise choice to overindulge himself on alcoholic beverages. He was quite a disgrace.

Chapter 5

A Place of Despair

I remarried in 2015 and my husband and I worked twixt and between the UK and abroad to help to fund my sons through university. Despite a large age gap, they both went at the same time and enjoyed four years in Edinburgh.

In August of 2019 I was fortunately in the UK. My eldest son told me that he was receiving imploring phone calls from a lady who worked in a hotel in the town where Marcus lived. My son was on a holiday in Prague, but the calls were persistent, she sounded desperate and the lady had convinced my son that he needed to visit his father immediately. She reported that she had had to throw him out of the hotel and not allow him in anymore. She believed that he had also been evicted from his accommodation. He was in a bad state. She said that she felt very sorry for him as he was well spoken and she believed that he had come from a good home and somehow fallen into this deplorable condition. He was clearly in need of help.

My husband booked an immediate flight for my son to the UK. It involved a change in Dusseldorf. He missed this and a further flight was paid for. I picked him up after midnight from Manchester and drove through the early hours to Devon. I had booked a room at the hotel the lady had called from. We arrived at 4am so a night porter let us in and we tried to sleep. After breakfast we set out to look for Marcus. We tried every hotel. They all knew him and reported that he was no longer allowed in the hotels. They expressed concern. We looked in all the cafes, the bars and the shops. Fortunately, it is only a small town. We found a charity cafe for homeless people and the kind gentleman there said we were welcome to take Marcus there for a shower and a cup of tea once we had found him. As we were leaving, we met two lovely ladies from the housing department who said they were also looking for Marcus. They were worried about him. We exchanged numbers and they said they would try to find him temporary accommodation, but they were having trouble as many places were refusing to take him. We bumped into them again in the town, still looking. They told us that from their office window they would watch Marcus when he went to the cashpoint to make sure that he was safe. We were quite touched by this kindness. It seemed that many people in the town were concerned for his welfare.

We had run out of places to look on foot, so we were driving around the streets. As we passed the park, we saw Marcus. He was sat on a bench just beside the road. We stopped the car and my son went to speak with him. Marcus spoke with him as though it was normal for him to be there. As he stood up we realised that he was not going to be able to get in the car; he was wearing shorts and his legs were covered in faeces. He seemed completely oblivious to this fact. He agreed to go with us to the café and have a shower. It was a shock to see him in this emaciated state. As you might imagine, this was quite devastating for my son. Marcus used to be quite a robust figure of fifteen or sixteen stone; he looked very old and frail and weighed possibly less than ten stone. We understood the urgency with which the lady from the hotel had called. He wasn't able to recognise that he needed to wash, dress, eat or find accommodation. He was unable to facilitate any of these things and did not look likely to survive living outside for long. He was very weak, could barely walk or speak coherently and could only be described as completely incapacitated. He was in quite a horrific state and it was very distressing to witness. He needed to be in care.

We helped him to shuffle to the café and my son showered his father. He gave him his own clothes to wear and wore some himself from a scrap bag. I bought 'nappies' from the nearby chemist and told Marcus he must put one on. Marcus told me that he was banned from the chemist shop as they thought he was shoplifting. He might be alcoholic but I'm sure he's not a thief. He must have been getting into some pretty bad states.

Time was short as we only had this day and the following day; I needed to return to Yorkshire the day after that. I phoned a number for social services to see if anyone could help. The lady I spoke with was very abrupt, with no sympathy at all for this predicament. She told me that Marcus' condition was of his own making and that social services did not help in these cases; that was the end of that. I phoned the housing department and they were still struggling to find accommodation for him for that night. I phoned the doctors' surgery and took an emergency appointment. I tried the social services again, I explained that he was an old man in desperate need of help. The lady told me that he was not old and that she had much older clients to support. This was ridiculous, Marcus was a pensioner aged sixty-seven; he was clearly not young or middle-aged and he was in desperate need of help. I was almost pleading, but to no avail. What had become of inter-agency collaboration I wondered and why do we have social services if they are unwilling to service those in a state of utmost desperation? The lady gave me the impression that she had decided that this man was undeserving. Who was she to make this decision? This only served to demonstrate to me the complete lack of empathy and education about the condition of alcoholism. Within professional services I expected more.

We walked across the town to the medical centre. The doctor did not have much sympathy either. Looking at the state that Marcus was in I found this quite awful. However, in his defence, it transpired that the doctor had admitted Marcus to hospital the previous week and he had discharged himself; I expect he felt that there was little he could do that he hadn't already tried. I asked if it was possible to section Marcus as he was clearly a danger to himself and would not survive for long living outside without accommodation. The doctor was of the same view as social services that he had brought it on himself and was choosing this as a life choice. The doctor referred Marcus to the hospital again.

I don't know anything about addiction but surely if a person is an addict, then by definition, they are ill and not able to make the choice to say no to the toxic substance. I am learning more as I write this book! There must be a difference between 'I would like a drink' and 'I must have a drink'. I do not think that this is even a matter of being able to say 'no'. A person who is alcoholic is not declining any offer, they are deliberately going in search of alcohol. Maybe they cannot say 'no' to themselves and to their inner voice which is instructing them to go in search.

You will read more research from 1881 further in this book. My view above is only that of a layman, but surprisingly, it is in perfect accordance with some research I subsequently found from a Doctor Mann in 1881 who stated:

> "*We must distinguish between an incontrollable and intermittent impulse to take alcoholic stimulant … and the physiological state in which the individual merely chooses to indulge in liquor to excess. The great question of importance is to distinguish the two states or conditions, when the result – inebriety – is the same.*" (Mann, 1881)

Both social services and the doctor told me that Marcus was choosing to drink. How are professional services ignorant of this information which has been around for nearly a century and a half when it is blatantly obvious to me that Marcus is in the first state?

Furthermore, a quick search on Google tells me that if a person abruptly stops drinking, the body suffers painful effects such as shaking, insomnia, nausea and increased anxiety. Without some external help is a person able to go through this process? I think that by this time it is too late to say that a person is choosing to drink. They have chosen to start drinking in the past but by this stage they are physically and mentally unable to just stop. Refusing to help a person in this situation has no other outcome than condemnation to chronic ill health and social problems. Unless the person dies, these health and social problems will later have to be picked up by the health and social services. Surely, prevention would be better than cure.

We drove Marcus to the hospital and admitted him. He was certainly not able to make any choices at all. We picked up a small rucksack from the hotel which they kept for Marcus. It had a bottle of gin in it and a phone. Marcus had lost his wallet, so he had no money or access to any, no clothes and no accommodation; he had no control of his bowels and was unaware that this was an issue – who would make this as a life choice?

The hospital staff were amazing; I don't know how they do it. We had a nurse who was very firm but kind. My son was struggling not to cry most of the time. The nurse asked Marcus to look at him and see the grief he was causing. Marcus refused to look round. At one point I left the room. Despite being told how desperately ill he was, Marcus asked his son for the bottle of gin he had in his rucksack. We had already poured it away.

Marcus was given food, which he ate heartily and cups of tea. We told the housing department that he didn't need accommodation for that night, then we left him in the evening and said we would be back in the morning. We went to buy him a set of clean clothes. It had been a very harrowing and tiring day.

The next morning, we returned to the hospital. We were told that he would need to 'dry out'. The nurse explained that Marcus would need to be on drugs to ease the process of alcohol withdrawal. It was clear that he would not be leaving for a while.

Marcus was delighted with his new clothes and thought he would be leaving. I was worried that he would discharge himself again. I asked if he understood why he was there. He told me that he thought that his salt levels were a little high. I was quite angry and asked him to try again. He said that maybe he had drunk too much. I am not a psychologist and was really at a loss as to how much he was conscious of his predicament; at that time I don't think he was conscious of it at all. He just wanted another drink. As he was able to change his reasoning from saying that he was not in hospital due to alcohol-related causes to that he was, I can only conclude that he probably spent most of his life in denial of his addiction. I feel that underneath he did really know what the problem was, but refused to acknowledge it to anyone or maybe even to himself. It was like a compulsive liar believing his own lies. I found research to support my thoughts on this:

> "Denial of an addiction to alcohol to a second party may be associated with the individual having a conscious awareness of their problem." (Dyson, 2007 in RCP CR185, 2014)

This behaviour may be due to a natural defence mechanism; alcoholics can become very wily in their endeavours to convince others that they are not drinking. My current husband has told me of his ex-father-in-law who would repeatedly top up a lager can with gin and tonics after consuming the lager and would assert emphatically that he was drinking 'just the one' lager, despite evidence to the contrary of the smell of gin and even having watched him top up the can through the kitchen window, with gin he had stashed in a cupboard. The somewhat inaccurate catchphrase 'just the one' was used by Mrs Wembley in the popular TV series 'On the Up' when asked if a small tipple would be agreeable. The overindulgence was a source of humour in the programme. Again, this is something that we take for granted as humour; it is culturally humorous to have 'one too many'.

The denial of 'drinking too much' may also be due to not wanting anyone to know that consumption is a problem which has 'got out of hand'. This would necessitate admitting to 'not being able to hold your liquor'. Who would want to admit that? Certainly, no self-respecting Scotsman or even an 'honorary' one such as Marcus.

In Marcus' condition in a hospital bed, I assumed that his inability to understand or communicate information effectively, was due to the decline of mental condition he was in. His contesting of any suggestion that he was alcoholic was well versed and came as naturally as a muscle memory. My son stayed with him for most of the day and finally we had to leave.

I returned home still worried that he would discharge himself. My sons and myself phoned daily to check on his progress. I explained that he would be homeless if they let him go and they said they wouldn't let him leave without somewhere to go to and that they would advise security that he was not to leave. I felt reassured.

I believe that he stayed in the hospital for quite a length of time and was then admitted to a secure home for people with dementia in the autumn of 2019. My sons visited him and reported that he was putting on weight and was being well looked after. They were very pleased with his progress and allowed to take him out, but if he drank at all in this time then he would not be readmitted. He of course asked them to buy alcohol; he asked them for a bottle of gin for Christmas, making all manner of excuses as to how the home would be fine with this. This indicated to me that he was completely unaware of the consequences that had resulted in his confinement. Although he did not want to be confined, he had not understood how he came to be in such a situation and would readily repeat it. He was an intelligent man who seemed to have lost any ability to reason or understand cause and effect. After months of abstention from alcohol how had his brain not recovered enough to enable him to comprehend what had happened to him? If questioned face to face, he would seemingly give correct answers, but we knew that in his head, he was only being devious, and that, given any opportunity at all, he would go in search of the next drink. He would say that he didn't want to be in a home and that he understood that if he drank he would have to be in a home. However, with the mentality of a three-year old, he did not actually understand at all. His brain was completely addled.

As my younger son pointed out, he was also completely unaware of the anguish that he was causing, especially to his eldest son. At what point had he lost all capacity for empathy, even for his own son? He had been a kind and caring man, well able to and regularly demonstrating compassion for and understanding of, the feelings of others. Yet, despite his apparent improvement in mental and physical health, it was as if his brain had turned to mush. It still only craved alcohol to the exception of all else. Thankfully, he was not allowed out on his own. He had been very well looked after and gained in strength and weight, but unfortunately, it seemed, also in 'mental capacity'.

After less than a year in care at the secure home for those with dementia he was clearly feeling better. He complained that he didn't want to be there and that he had no internet access. My sons bought him a laptop. Apparently, a social worker was helping to orchestrate his 'escape'. I wrote to the home to explain his long-term addiction and to detail the horrific condition he had been in the year before and to beseech them not to let him leave. In September of 2020 he told my eldest son that he had never been much of a drinker and asked my younger son to help him look for alternative accommodation as he *'had to have hope'*. He was referring to hope to get out of his confinement, but I know that secretly it was hope that he could have another drink. How anyone could actually believe that he could live independently without alcohol after drinking daily and heavily for maybe forty years I don't know. Maybe it was easy to be deceived by his words of contrition and repentance and his no doubt assurances that he would be a reformed man. However, I know that whilst these words tripped easily off his silver tongue, he was plotting where to buy his first bottle. He thought he was clever.

Maybe he was. In the summer of 2020, my eldest son was living in Australia, I too was abroad and my youngest son was in Scotland. My youngest son had a call from someone from the Deprivation of Liberty Safeguards Service who asked if he would be willing to advocate on behalf of his father to help him to leave the home. Of course, he would not. In December, I received correspondence from her too. She asked if she could use the details of the information I had written to the home. I consented of course and advised very strongly that it would be certainly against Marcus' best interests that he be allowed to leave the home where he was being so well cared for and returning to good health; he almost certainly would start drinking again. It was a waste of time.

By March of 2021 he had been to court and the judge decreed that he had 'mental capacity'. He moved to a less secure home with 24-hour care which offered a 'pathway to independence'. This was not what he had wanted but it only took him a month before he managed to convince everyone that he was fit enough to leave. He left in April and told my sons that he was a free man again. Our hearts sank.

Chapter 6

Full Circle Again

My eldest son came home on holiday with his girlfriend and wanted to visit his father. It was the summer of 2022 and Marcus was seventy years old. Eighteen months had passed since Marcus had left the home for dementia patients and he had been free to choose his own accommodation and was ruled fit to make his own decisions. My son phoned his father to suggest that he visit the following week. With slight trepidation he wanted to introduce him to his girlfriend. Marcus told him that unfortunately he would be in Greece with a lady friend who was paying for the holiday for him. He was due to leave the next day. This seemed rather odd and unbelievable. Neither of my sons had heard about this lady before or of a trip to Greece. They 'smelled a rat'. Fortunately, my son and his girlfriend did not travel to Devon.

The following week when Marcus would have supposedly been in Greece, he phoned my son and asked if he would take him to the bank to withdraw some money. My son was in the North of Scotland and Marcus was in Devon! My son pointed out this fact and that he had said that he would be in Greece. Marcus apologised and said he had forgotten. I am not sure how a person can forget something that never happened; my sons have never lived in Devon and how could you forget to go on a holiday to Greece?

Once again, I questioned the notion of 'having mental capacity' as being applicable to Marcus. How could anyone rule that this man had 'mental capacity'? I admit that he is an intelligent man and very able to put a good argument in his defence. He has always been a good speaker and able to be very convincing. However, he clearly had little idea of what he was doing; he couldn't remember where his sons were living and remembered very little of what he was told or what he had told others. This behaviour was of course very worrying.

My youngest son, now having taken up the mantle of 'emergency contact' as my oldest son and myself had been abroad, phoned social services to advise them of his current behaviour. More phone calls followed from Marcus to my youngest son asking him to get shopping for him. Marcus told my youngest son about a lady who was with him and that he could speak to her on FaceTime. However, when he turned to see her, she had gone. My son wondered if this lady was real or imaginary. He was clearly slipping or had slipped down some slope again. On another occasion he told my son that his friend and billionaire 'Anthony Blunt' had helped him to get out of his care home. I wondered if had been watching 'The Crown' and had somehow written himself into the story or how he might have mixed up his own life with that of the notorious art historian and double agent. The following day he phoned my son and asked him to take him to an enquiry. My son, being over four hundred miles away, asked what this was about. Marcus replied that he and Anthony Blunt must attend an enquiry or else they would be in big trouble and that they needed to leave immediately. My son told him that there was no enquiry and that of course he would not be taking him. These calls were quite disturbing and how is anyone to know what to do?

My son had received some communication from social services so I said I would email them with the current situation and advise them of his strange phone calls. He was talking gibberish and clearly had resumed his excessive alcohol consumption. I asked if they would visit him as I felt he was in danger. I received a detailed reply and told that a visit would be scheduled. My son tried to follow this up, the visit was not forthcoming. Apparently, Marcus had been put on a list.

Two months later my son received a phone call from the police. Marcus had been evicted from his accommodation. He is now, as I write, in hospital telling the nurses that his sons are policemen (which they are not). The nurse told my son that he was maybe suffering from alcohol induced psychosis.

My friend kindly went to visit Marcus. She had not met him previously. She reported that he was quite charming, clearly a cultured and well-educated man and that he was able to relate many stories in a lucid and articulate manner. Ones from his past had accurate details, such as the college he attended when he left school, that his sister was a teacher, and where he had lived. Their initial conversation would have led her to believe that there was nothing wrong with him until the conversation continued. It was easy to see how a court, she said, could have been easily deceived into believing that Marcus was fully compos mentis. His more recent memories, however, were delusional. He related to my friend that his sons were policemen, which she knew they were not. Additionally, one son had spoken to him only a few hours earlier and corrected him on this point, which showed that he was unable to retain information even between morning and afternoon. According to Marcus, one son and his lawyer had been shot and were recovering in hospital, the second son was in charge of a sting operation and had co-opted the help of the Cornish police force. I was dead, due to an overdose as my husband had left me. He was very adamant that these 'facts' were true. He was clearly existing in an alternate reality, created by his inability to retain short term memories and his muddling of his real and fictional experiences, maybe from TV. He told my son earlier that the reason he was in hospital was *'due to a series of unfortunate events which unfolded'*. My son told him that he was actually in hospital because he was alcoholic. Marcus hung up. I can now view this behaviour from a different perspective and consider that maybe this is what happened to him at work in the past and that when he was given information that conflicted with his inaccurate memories, he was given to believe that people were deliberately trying to confuse him. This is eminently possible.

The following day my friend took him some juice that he had requested. More fanciful stories were forthcoming, and my sons had been promoted to inspectors. Many people, his old friends included, had been imprisoned. I saw analogies in his stories – I had for obvious reasons had been killed off; the man in the next bed and his elder son who had argued with him the previous day had both been shot and old friends who had deserted him had been imprisoned. It is possible to see how these scenarios had been played out in his muddled mind. He did however, relate factual information from his past, his school and early life and the meal he made me of sole bon femme; he even recalled that it had accompanying broccoli! This meal clearly had a huge impact on both of us!

Marcus' current mental condition had deteriorated considerably, although his physical state was better than when I met him three years ago. I am sure that this deterioration could have been averted if only 'the professionals' had a greater awareness of and understanding of his condition and he had been able to benefit from high quality treatment in a specialised centre for alcoholics. The services available seemed blind to his condition and the legislation did nothing to ensure his safety or to support his recovery.

Three years ago, the diligence of the lady in the hotel, who I feel was responsible for saving Marcus' life (the book is dedicated to her), our trip to rescue him and get him to hospital, the excellent work of the hospital staff and those at the care home, were completely negated by social services and a judge who declared him to have mental capacity, resulting in a recurrent scenario three years on.

Where is the point when the services available are seemingly working against each other? Or is it a point in this case, of the law simply *'being an ass'*?

Section Three

Chapter 7

Seeking Answers

Where did it go wrong? I know now that Marcus was alcoholic when I met him. I was blissfully unaware of this at the time and assumed that anyone alcoholic would be rolling around in the streets being abusive. This was not the man I knew at all. He was gregarious, cultured, confident and generous.

What caused his perception of the world however, in which heavy, daily alcoholic consumption was normal? How did Marcus not see for himself that his behaviour and that of his friends, married with children, when I met him, was not the same as his own and that his insistence that 'everybody drinks' was certainly not at the same level as his? Why did he so vigorously seek to delude himself that all was OK?

To my mind, it starts as self-deception. It is a selfishness, self-indulgence, maybe simply for pleasure or response to an inability to cope with life. It becomes self-gratification above concern for all others. For a man so caring and generous, how could Marcus become so overwhelmed with the desire to satisfy his craving for alcohol, that he allowed it to ruin his marriage, his family and his life? Surely, no-one of right mind would do this consciously.

How is a judge able to rule that a man who is so clearly incapable of deciding not to put alcohol to his lips, based on a wealth of historical evidence, has the mental capacity to make decisions about his care? I will explore possible answers to these questions in the next two chapters. The judge must know, as anyone would, that as soon as this man is able, he will choose to drink. Apparently, that is his right. But is it morally right that if a man is so seriously ill, as to be unable to make that decision, that he should be deemed so and allowed to put his life in the gravest danger for a second time? The cost of council services should also be a consideration too. Marcus had taken up the time and cost of police, doctors, nurses, social workers and housing department administrators. Indeed, the lady I first spoke to from the social services department was completely unwilling to devote any time to a man who deliberately sought to destroy himself. She thought that other people were more deserving of help; there is a finite amount of service to go round.

How is this man's behaviour even reasonable for the society in which he lives? He has adversely affected all the hoteliers in his town; he has no doubt lined their pockets too at their invitation. He has taken up police services on a regular basis and he told me one time, that the police were his friends and that they came to take him home in the evening. It seems he convinced himself that they were a friendly taxi service and lost all sense of reality of the purpose of the police force or why they may have been called to remove him from premises. Is this not an indication that the man is not of sound mind? He had, in fact, lost all ability to reason. I assume that he had upset other customers in the hotels and bars he had frequented. He had upset those he had been accommodated by. Despite all this, his town wanted to help him. Each place my son and I visited expressed a desire to help him. Did they see something of the Marcus he used to be? He has rejected any help. I know that anyone who has reported his behaviour has then become his enemy (in his head) when in fact they have been trying to get him help. He has always refused to help himself and refused to acknowledge that he needed help.

There is no question that he has caused his own near demise, but he has not consciously taken a decision to nearly kill himself; he has gradually over fifty or more years deteriorated to this point. He does not want to be ill. He has subconsciously trained his body to have a high tolerance for large quantities of alcohol. He has been able to function, to work for over thirty years, to have a family and maintain a good standard of living.

At what point does a person 'become' alcoholic? To the layman, such as myself, I would say 'at the point at which one is dependent'. But who is to say when that point occurs? Is it up to the individual to self-assess that point and to seek help? I suspect so. If, when I met him, Marcus knew that he had reached that point, which he probably did, as he sought to conceal it; he did not want or was not willing to do anything about it. Then, at that point there is no issue (one can't see the future consequence). He was fit and healthy and enjoying his life. One cannot see either the condition of the brain and extrapolate the possible toll that alcohol will have on the brain, nor estimate the complete havoc it will wreak in later life. A person does not have the benefit of hindsight. Maybe he should have been bright enough, sensible enough, concerned enough to know what was happening or what would happen, to be able to be introspective, to be able to take control of himself. Maybe if he had lived in America and had the benefit of a weekly therapy session, he would have spoken about it and realised the damage he was causing to himself. He didn't. He more likely received adulation and praise for his 'capacity' to hold his drink, unconsciously, further fuelling his downward spiral. If he was aware of his condition (which I suspect that he was), he certainly was not willing to open up about it, to discuss it, or to divulge any concerns that he had and most certainly not to admit to it. He would fiercely condemn anyone who sought to contradict him about his non dependence upon alcohol. It was as if someone might take away his dummy and he was not going to give it up. He would fight for it at all and any cost.

If Marcus was alcoholic when I met him and is alcoholic now at what point was there a change in his ability to function? There is clearly a point at which he went from being a high functioning alcoholic (a possibly respectable term) to just an alcoholic (a pitiful and derisory term). I suspect that the change occurred when the alcohol damaged his brain to the extent that it was not able to recover and he became unable to function at the level that was required of him. I don't know if this is a long or a short process or whether or not it is the same for all individuals or indeed if there was a specific time that it happened.

What then is alcoholism? Is it an illness? Are there levels of alcoholism? Is there a sliding scale of alcoholicness? Although this is not a real word it seems an appropriate one here to describe the propensity to consume alcohol. It seems from this story that maybe there is.

This man has slid further down into incapacity over forty or fifty years. I don't know that Marcus had been subject to any assessment, certainly not when I was with him but there is a tool which poses questions relating to behaviour and seeks to determine whether the extent of alcoholism is mild, moderate or severe.

This assessment tool is used for the diagnosis of Alcohol Use Disorder (AUD) and is to be found in the Diagnostic and Statistical Manual of Mental Disorders, Fifth Edition (DSM-5) published in 2013 (NIAAA[2]). It integrates the terms 'alcohol abuse' and 'alcohol dependence' into the term 'alcohol use disorder' which is synonymous with the term 'alcoholism'. It was devised in order to collect statistical data in the USA. It presents a series of eleven questions, relating to difficulties with making a choice to resist alcohol, difficulties with daily functioning or subsequent health issues because of alcohol. It effectively looks at how alcohol consumption is affecting a person's life. If a person is in a position where they are able to undertake this assessment, then maybe they are also in a position to decide to take action to make some positive changes. I believe that Marcus was already beyond this point when I met him.

The presence of two out of the eleven criteria indicates the existence of AUD. If two or three of the criteria applied over the previous year, then this indicates a mild level of severity, four or five symptoms indicate a moderate level of severity and if six or more of the criteria applied then the level is classed as severe. It relies of course, also on the respondent giving truthful answers. I suspect that if anyone had administered the test to Marcus, he would have ensured that his answers showed that he was if a drinker at all, then it would only be at a mild level of severity.

This behavioural assessment tool does not measure any physical damage to the brain that might subsequently affect the ability of the respondent to answer the questions; maybe that would necessitate a brain scan.

Also, each of the eleven criterion does not have equal weighting with the others in their ability to assess the severity of abuse (Boness et al., 2019). For example, one person might exhibit only three criteria as opposed to another who exhibits five, but the person exhibiting three may actually be in a more serious condition than the one exhibiting five. It is clearly a very complex area. Based on the work of Boness and colleagues, a new research-based framework in 2022 has been developed which focusses on thirteen risk factors rather than on the consequences of actions, to identify profiles of risk to enable intervention at early stages.

Having assessed a person's behaviour in respect of their relationship with alcohol what then defines that person as alcoholic?

How is understanding of this condition so little that social services to my mind would dismiss anyone in his condition and determine that he chose to be in this state? Help was refused when requested but when the man was back to good health, social services sought to place him back to the place from whence he came! I fail to see how anyone could do this. Even if the law said so, I find it hard to believe that one human being would deliberately help another to become so ill. I am sure that the people involved were acting in good faith and according to law and guidelines. But to my mind, it doesn't seem right.

Maybe he should have helped himself, but how does a person in denial, decide that he needs help? Is denial conscious and deliberate? I understand that in order to receive help from organisations such as Alcoholics Anonymous one must own up to being alcoholic. Some people can and do. I wonder how far down the slippery slope they have slid before they manage to do this and what if anything, finally motivates them to be able to seek help. If a person does not have the capacity to do that due to the condition of being alcoholic what is the next recourse? The questions seem never-ending.

To answer the question of how alcoholism may be defined I have referred to some research:

Edenberg and Foroud (2013) describe alcoholism as *'a maladaptive pattern of excessive drinking leading to serious problems.'*

A maladaptive pattern means that the individual is not able to adjust their behaviour appropriate to the current situation. In other words, the person is unable to modify their behaviour, for example to decide to leave a social gathering early or decide that two drinks one evening might be enough or even, none at all.

What might be considered as excessive? Is there an acceptable level? The NHS currently advises no more than 14 units per week. One unit as a very rough guide is:

Half a pint of lager/beer/cider = 275ml (ABV 3.6%)

A measure of spirit = 25ml (ABV 40%)

A small glass of wine = 125ml (ABV 12%)

ABV = Average by volume = percentage per litre. For example, 40% means 40ml of alcohol per litre.

Marcus used to drink 500ml cans of Carlsberg Special Brew when I first knew him, which used to have an ABV of 9%, nearly double that of a regular beer which had an ABV of 5%. Each can contained 4.5 units of alcohol. Today's recommendation would mean that four cans in a week would be the limit. In 2015 Carlsberg reduced the volume of Special Brew to 7.5% (approximately 2 units) in an effort to appeal to a more 'health-conscious' market (The Secret History of Special Brew, 2015).

According to a report by the Institute of Alcohol Studies (IAS, undated), in 1987 the recommendation was no more than 21 units for men and 14 for women per week. In five days Marcus would have exceeded this if he only drank one can per day. He drank considerably more than that every day. In 1995 types of drinker were categorised into moderate (less than 21 units per week), hazardous (21-50 units per week) and harmful (50+ units per week). Fifty units would be eleven cans per week. I imagine that Marcus would easily have consumed four cans of lager per night putting him well into the 'harmful' category. In 2016 the recommendation became 14 units for men and women. Research now shows that Marcus was drinking at dangerously high levels. He was consuming a weekly limit in an evening. Neither did he ever have the recommended two to three days' abstinence in between. This habitual pattern had been persistent for twenty years and that was over twenty years ago. Marcus' drinking had certainly been excessive. According to the definition from Edenberg and Foroud and contrary to my solicitor's view Marcus was certainly alcoholic when I sought to divorce him in 2002.

Information from Elkins, (2020) defines alcoholism as:

> *"a chronic disease of the brain that's characterised by compulsive decision-making, impulsive behaviour and relapse. It's triggered by generic and environmental factors, and it causes biological changes in the brain that make abstaining from alcohol nearly impossible without medical treatment."*

Again, the definition of alcoholism infers that the person suffering from this condition is compelled to consume alcohol and is unable to control or resist the craving. This definition goes further by explaining that this is due to changes in the brain caused by excessive consumption.

Elkins, (2020) also advises that a chronic disease:

- Lasts for a long time
- Is caused by multiple factors
- Cannot be prevented by vaccine
- Cannot be cured by medication
- Requires ongoing medical attention

In Marcus' case the disease has lasted over forty years so that certainly qualifies it as a chronic disease.

What are the multiple factors that cause alcoholism? Is it hereditary, is it born of anxiety, grief, or major life changes? There are many questions I have posed to myself which I expect are the same for others living with people suffering from alcoholism. Kendler et al., (2011) suggest that possible causes include genetic, psychological and environmental factors. These are root causes but the actions that cause a person to become alcoholic are regular drinking and heavy drinking. I believe that the combination of these two factors cause a person to become alcohol dependent.

I have considered why a person may want to drink alcohol and suggest that it can induce a feeling of happiness, reduce anxiety, increase confidence and that it lowers inhibitions. It can help people to feel carefree and less concerned with daily worries. It can help people to feel more sociable and relaxed and possibly more able to sleep than they were previously. Additionally, research from Morikawa (2011) found that repeated exposure to alcohol affects the learning and memory areas of the brain such that the imbiber becomes increasingly receptive to learning. The subconscious mind serves to enhance alcohol-related experiences such as meals, music and people. The addict becomes addicted not to the pleasure experienced by the alcohol, but to the 'experience of the moment', including the environment, behaviour and physiological cues. These feelings are reinforced when alcohol triggers the release of dopamine in the brain.

In this euphoric state it is possibly difficult to consider the negative consequences. There are however, many negative effects: a person may feel vulnerable, due to suffering from lack of co-ordination, concentration and focus; a person may suffer diminished abilities, both mentally and physically, may lack judgement and the ability to make reasoned decisions and may suffer impotence; and they may become dopey or aggressive and their speech may become slurred and their ability to balance may be compromised. These are in fact the consequences that give rise to humour from the point of view of an observer, so could easily be viewed as positive if the drunk desired to be entertaining. Even in a sober state many people are unconcerned as to the detrimental effects of alcohol consumption, as generally they are not permanent if consumption is not heavy over an extended period of time.

Thankfully, aggression was not a consequence of alcohol consumption in Marcus' case. He tended more to get sociable and dopey when under the influence.

The problem with enjoying the effects of alcohol consumption is that they can come at the cost of wanting to repeat the experience regularly. Does this make the problem a psychological or an environmental one or is it simply down to the fact that the person finds it enjoyable and wishes to continue? As mentioned previously, Marcus managed to repeat this experience daily due to his many interests and association with other single friends who could do the same and he had the financial wherewithal to do it. Where those with family commitments were not able to keep up this pace, Marcus was able to continue to behave almost like at teenager, in his social habits, well into his thirties. His increasing tolerance of alcohol due to regular consumption also led to his consumption of greater quantities, in order to achieve the same level of 'positive' effects. It is maybe prudent to remember that Marcus believed that he was functioning well and that there was no problem. In the years that I lived with him he was generally in good health; he maintained a high level of fitness through daily attendance at a gym and participated in many sports; he had a voracious appetite and ate a varied and healthy diet. He was never ill, that I recall, and we used to joke that he had the constitution of an ox. However, I think that age takes its toll. To whatever extent a healthy diet and exercise can ameliorate the effects of excessive alcohol consumption, it cannot do so forever; this level of abuse to one's brain and body cannot be maintained indefinitely without severe detrimental consequences.

The next question I have pondered and investigate answers to here, is that of predisposition to alcoholism. Maybe it was hereditary, or are there other factors which may predispose a person to alcohol dependence?

A predisposition doesn't necessarily cause a disease to develop but can contribute to its development. History of family alcohol misuse can be a contributory factor. Marcus' mother told me that his father was probably alcoholic. This increases his risk of developing a drinking problem to approximately 50% (Slaughter et al., 2022). There could be three contributory factors to Marcus' dependence – environment (social pressure and opportunity), psychological (simple desire to continue and/or underlying mental issues) and genetics (as purported by Kendler, 2011).

Edenberg and Foroud (2013) state that there is an abundance of evidence that alcoholism is a complex genetic disease. However, there is no alcoholism gene and only genes which throughout families indicate a predisposition to alcoholism.

Interestingly, Edenberg and Foroud (2013) also explained that there are alleles* (the parts of a gene which determine specific traits) which help to deter individuals from excessive alcoholic consumption.

People with these alleles experience facial flushing, tachycardia (a faster than normal heartbeat of over 100 beats per minute) and nausea when they consume alcohol.

The existence in the body of one of these alleles is prevalent in the East Asian community but almost non-existent in individuals of European descent. A person with one of these alleles, therefore has some degree of protection against becoming dependent upon alcohol. In Edenberg and Foroud's research they note that societal circumstances were found to be able to override this protective effect when there was social pressure to drink. This would indicate that social factors are a stronger influence on alcoholic consumption than genetics.

However, where an individual carries two copies of the allele its influence is more effective and renders the individual almost unable to consume alcohol. There is medication which replicates this effect and is used to help alcoholics in recovery.

It seems that Europeans have a predisposition to becoming alcoholic which may be genetic and compounded by social and environmental factors. It is a combination of these factors which results in a person becoming or not becoming alcoholic.

The study of epigenetics is an area which examines how environmental factors and a person's behaviour can affect how genes respond. It suggests that behaviour and environment can effectively turn on or off the way that a person's genes work. Therefore, a person who has a predisposition to alcoholism because there is a family history of alcoholism may, due to environmental and behavioural factors have no disposition which results in them turning to alcohol. Conversely, a person with little genetic predisposition to alcoholism can become alcoholic due to external pressure from their social environmental such that it has an overriding influence on a person's choice of behaviours (National Institute on Drug Abuse, 2019).

After ascertaining that it was possible that Marcus inherited part of a gene which predisposed him to alcohol dependency, my next question is whether or not Marcus was under social pressure to drink. It is possible that behaviour and environment could have contributed to the triggering of his genetic disposition to alcoholism. I expect that Marcus was under social pressure to drink. As a teenager and student, it is possible that this was the case. He was a student longer than many and did not complete his degree and postgraduate qualification until maybe two to three years after the usual three or four years.

Most certainly as part of a rugby team (which he was from adolescence), there is an expectation that members will drink quite heavily. However, there is also an expectation that players will be fit and healthy and certainly not intoxicated prior to, or during a game. The heavy drinking was post matches and even these were possibly curtailed by the fact that matches were held on a Sunday and the players had to recover enough to go to work on a Monday. It was part of the bravado of team members that they could hold their liquor and Sunday afternoons are often enjoyed in an alcoholic haze. This said, not all rugby players are alcoholic and probably most are very fit and healthy. It was possibly a contributory factor but not a specific cause. I suspect that the drinking of the rugby team was limited to a couple of times per week. This was not of course the case with Marcus. When I first met him, he had other social gatherings throughout his week which would involve alcohol consumption. It was obviously more enjoyable to have a drink with friends than to drink alone at home. This also provided an acceptable cover for his drinking behaviour and each social grouping only saw him consuming alcohol at the time they spent with him. It was the same for me, I was not at any of the sports club evening gatherings; I saw him a couple of times a week which would usually involve a meal and the obligatory accompanying drinks. Of course, with regard to choice, Marcus was choosing to be in environments where consuming alcohol was the norm or expected. Was he really choosing at that time or had his dependency already taken hold and was guiding his decisions? In concurrence with Kendler's findings it would appear to be possible that all three factors of genetics, environment and psychological together may have influenced Marcus' likelihood of becoming addicted to alcohol.

According to information from Buddy (2020), individuals in their early to mid-twenties are most at risk from alcohol abuse. Those who start drinking before the age of fifteen are most likely to become alcoholic in later life.

Marcus came from a middle-class family with caring parents. It is possible that alcohol was always in the home, so in that sense available, but I do not believe that he was encouraged to drink alcohol regularly before the age of fifteen. Information from Matrix Diagnostics (Matrix News, 2020) suggests that this is maybe still the case for around 20% of children aged ten to fifteen at Christmas. Marcus told me that he used to be given advocaat at Christmas, maybe once he was in secondary school. I remember having it myself too as a Christmas treat. There was even a TV advert which had the jingle 'Eveninks and morninks, I drink Warninks'. This clearly and shockingly, advocated having an alcoholic drink at any time of day! I think that at Christmas some children were possibly given a 'Snowball' which was advocaat diluted with lemonade and lime juice. It was certainly more acceptable and probably common to do this in the 1960s and people were not aware of long-term harmful effects to the brain as a result of alcohol consumption.

Of significant interest is that in 1881 Edward Mann, (MD) in New York proposed that a predisposition to dipsomania (a historical term for alcoholism) was likely hereditary and that it possibly gains in intensity through generations, such that once a person tastes intoxicating liquors and begins to indulge in them, then they are hooked.

Concurrent with the suggested causes so far, the National Institute on Alcohol Abuse and Alcoholism (NIAAA[1]) website advises that:

- Heavy drinking in adolescence predicts future AUD
- Between 50% and 60% of vulnerability to AUD is inherited

It also offers further indicators of predisposition to alcoholism which include:

- Environment
- Childhood trauma

- Stress
- Mental health issues

In Marcus' case I have proposed specific environments which have been contributory – student life, sport (especially rugby) and a wide social life. High pressure work environments are suggested in the literature, but I cannot imagine that a college library can be in this category.

Childhood trauma is a possible cause. Maybe the death of his father at an early age was sufficient trauma to trigger an initial need for an external crutch in his teenage years. Although I am sure that there are other children who lost parents at an early age who do not become alcoholic. Yang et al. (2002) suggest that disadvantageous life circumstances such as this can provide possible causes but certainly factors such as neglect, abuse or an impoverished background certainly do not apply in Marcus' case. Yang et al. also cite divorce as a causal factor which of course may have further exacerbated his already fragile condition in 2002.

Stress seems to be a possible cause, as Marcus seemed stressed at work. I think this was more to do with his relationship with people or his own personality than the environment of his work. But my observations are simply conjecture. How is anyone to know the full complement of factors in play over seventy years?

A person's mental health may be also attributable to predisposition, like genetics this is an extremely complex area. How a person feels and behaves is partly related to personality as well as their ability to deal with external influences. People who are less inhibited than others, want to be the 'life and soul of the party' or are extremely shy might believe that alcohol will help them to become more personable, give them increased confidence and help them to cope better in social situations. Holding positive expectations about the effects of alcohol is also more likely to render a person likely to overindulge than if drinking has negative connotations. Such beliefs will be dependent upon an individual's personal experiences.

Personality and alcohol may have a two-way relationship. Whilst personality may affect the likelihood of consuming alcohol, the consumption of alcohol can effect changes in personality traits (Gmel et al., 2020). Gmel, et al. point to research which suggests that those who consumed alcohol in their study, were more sociable than abstainers. As alcohol enhances mood in extraverted individuals, they received greater rewards from drinking. This research resonates with Marcus' situation. He liked to drink to be sociable and he was very sociable when drinking.

The term given to the motivation for reward which is driven by a person's physiological state and their learned association with reward is 'incentive salience'. It can be a mechanism for developing AUD. It refers to a process whereby a person is driven by desire for the object (in this case alcohol) but also by the associations with it. For example, in the case of Marcus, his desire for alcohol may also be stimulated by an associated environment such as a public house, sports club or bar area; or a smell of alcohol on a coat or another person; the sight of people drinking (through a high street window, on a poster or a TV advert); or by the sight or even the thought of a particular person (a friend or drinking partner). If all these things can effectively drive a man to drink, then it is possible to see how it may be relatively impossible to resist all of them, without locking oneself in a room and turning off the TV. Even then the thought of these things is not something that can be turned off.

The term 'auto-suggestion' comes to mind for me here, thinking of how Marcus would actually convince himself of his own protestations, such as that he was not alcohol dependent and told his son that 'he was not much of drinker' after he had been in hospital for treatment for alcohol abuse. Through examples such as those outlined above, Marcus would always resort to confirmation bias to justify and normalise his actions. To some extent, he was right; according to a YouGov survey in 2021, 82% of people surveyed (sample size around 1500) over 18 years of age in the UK, reported that they drank alcohol, with 18% reporting that they did not. What Marcus was not able to reason outwardly (maybe he did, to himself) was the negative impact of alcohol upon his life or the fact that he drank more heavily than most people or over a more prolonged period of time than most people, with certainly less (or no) periods of abstention in between, than most people. He was always able to convince himself that what he was doing was OK and that it was the same as 'everyone' else and that there was no problem with that. He was unable to take on board anyone else's view of the same circumstances. I presume that this was his defence mechanism.

Another contributor to predisposition to alcoholism is mental illness. A person's inability to cope with daily issues and a low resilience to stress may result in turning to alcohol as a coping strategy for stress management. Stress may also induce an association with alcohol as a way of relieving the stress as a learned response, it dulls the senses and may incite a yearning for the sedative effect of alcohol in dulling any pain, mental or physical.

Mental health issues are very complex. I was not aware when I was with Marcus, of any diagnosed mental health issues although in the 1990s, I did question if Marcus was manic depressive (now identified as bi-polar) or suffering from some underlying mental disorder, due to his mood swings and inability to cope, and I suggested that he go to discuss this with his doctor. Again, in hindsight, this could have been the cause of his drinking or as a result of his drinking. Of course, he was always very reluctant to see a doctor in case he was asked about his drinking habits. He didn't go. Maybe his drinking was just an inappropriate coping mechanism for his inability to deal with daily life. He was in complete denial that his drinking was excessive or indeed problematic. He refused to see a doctor or indeed anyone who might question his compulsion to drink.

Referring back to Edenberg and Foroud's (2013) description of alcoholism as *'leading to serious problems'* I would question whose definition of 'serious problems' this would refer to. As Marcus was most of the time in denial, any problems resulting from his alcohol consumption were generally only to be determined by observers. This raises the question again of *'at what point does one become an alcoholic?'* How can this be determined? Over the forty years that I have known Marcus, has his excessive drinking been leading to serious problems? What may define a serious problem? His problems are now so serious that he can no longer live independently in my opinion. He is regularly denied private accommodation and is at serious risk of homelessness. He is indeed homeless at the moment of writing this and in hospital. At what point does anyone know where a person's habits are leading?

*An individual carries a particular gene to determine hair colour, the variation of that gene is called an allele and determines the specific colour.

Chapter 8

Alcohol, Detention, Mental Health and Capacity

The purpose of this chapter is to examine some of the legislation that is designed to help to keep individuals safe. It is examined in relation to mental health and alcohol consumption.

When a person is considered to be unable to make decisions to keep themselves safe from harm there are laws to help to protect them. Such decisions are not straightforward. For example, a person wishing to go climbing, sky-diving or any other extreme pursuit may be viewed as putting themselves in deliberate danger for the sake of an adrenaline rush, for sensory stimulation or to challenge themselves. However, precautions are usually taken to avert any serious risk of injury and the Health and Safety Act, (1974) covers organised activities and an amendment in 2016 – Adventure Activities Regulations, further legislated for safeguards to be in place. A person undertaking such activities can have some degree of comfort that precautions for their safety are undertaken.

Despite the detrimental effects of consuming alcohol, there is no legislation to prevent a person from over-indulging and this would be almost impossible as each person's level of tolerance is different based upon age, sex, size, fitness, body type, food consumed prior to consumption, amount consumed, previous times and length of times of consumption and period of abstention since the last consumption. This is probably not an exhaustive list.

There are little precautions to be taken, other than limiting the amount consumed and having periods of abstention in between bouts of drinking. This possible precautionary behaviour against becoming alcoholic, is what most sensible drinkers would conform to. In today's world we are well informed of the risks of alcoholic intake via all types of media. This was possibly not the case fifty years ago.

Autonomy - the freedom to make choices relating to oneself - is a human right under the UN Convention on the Rights of Persons with Disabilities (UN-CRPD, 2006); this includes persons with dementia which grants legal capacity regardless of their impairments (Wied et al., 2019). A person is free to partake of the drinks of their choosing. Every person also has a right to liberty.

There are circumstances in which a person can be deprived of these rights. The European Convention for Human Rights (ECHR) determines that a person has a right to liberty, except where they are to be detained in relation to a criminal offence, are illegally in a country or for purposes of education (for a child).

The Human Rights Act, 1998 incorporates the ECHR and Article 5, part 1e also allows:

> "the lawful detention of persons for the prevention of the spreading of infectious diseases, of persons of unsound mind, **alcoholics** or drug addicts or vagrants."

This act allows for the detention of alcoholics. This usually occurs because the drunk person is creating a public disturbance, which is governed by the Public Order Act of 1986. The proposed Bill of Rights Bill, introduced to Parliament in June, 2022 would repeal the Human Rights Act; it has not yet been enacted.

People can also be detained under the Mental Health Act, 1983 (amended in 2007). Section 3 is the part of the act referred to when a person is described as 'sectioned'. The Mental Health Act, Code of Practice advises that a person may be detained in hospital against their will for their own health or safety. When the person has been treated, they should then be free to leave.

A person can only be detained in a hospital or care home under the Mental Health Act. There is, however, the issue of protection from harm and where a person is acting in such a way as to be causing serious damage to themselves the concept of 'mental capacity' is central to determining whether treatment and care can be given to a person who refuses it. There is an acid test which states that:

> *"an individual who lacks the **capacity** to consent to the arrangements for their care and is subject to continuous supervision and control and is not free to leave their care setting is deprived of their liberty should be the subject of a DoLS application."*

The Liberty Protection Safeguards are part of the Mental Capacity Act (2005) and will supersede the Deprivation of Liberty Safeguards (DoLS).

The Mental Capacity Act, 2005 (MCA) is designed to protect people who lack the mental capacity to make their own decisions about their care and treatment. Section 2(a) states that:

> *"For the purposes of this Act, a person lacks capacity in relation to a matter if at the material time he is unable to make a decision for himself in relation to the matter because of an impairment of, or a disturbance in the functioning of the mind or brain."*

The Scottish equivalent of this act is the Adults with Incapacity (Scotland) Act 2000. Both acts enshrine five principles:

1.   Presumption of capacity unless proven otherwise.
2.   A person must be helped as much as possible to make their own decision.
3.   A person cannot be regarded as being unable to make a decision just because it is an unwise one.
4.   Any act or decision taken on behalf of a person who is deemed to lack capacity must be done in their best interests.
5.   Any act or decision taken on behalf of a person lacking mental capacity must be the least restrictive of their basic rights and freedoms. (CR185).

The MCA cannot be used to detain a person due to lack of mental capacity. The MCA complies with articles 5 and 8 of the ECHR (updated August, 2022). No person should be deprived of their liberty in an arbitrary fashion. Article 8 refers to the right to respect for private and family life. People have a right to freedom, to make their own decisions and to choose how to live their lives.

A person has a right to appeal against their deprivation of liberty. This is what happened in Marcus' case and it was deemed that he had mental capacity.

The two-stage test of mental capacity which is outlined in the Code of Practice seems clear:

- Does the person have an impairment of the mind or brain, or is there some sort of disturbance affecting the way their mind or brain works? (It doesn't matter whether the impairment or disturbance is temporary or permanent)
- If so, does that impairment or disturbance mean that the person is unable to make the decision in question at the time it needs to be made?

To my mind, Marcus in 2019 was suffering from a brain impairment which thwarted his ability to make decisions.

Under the auspices of the MCA are the Liberty Protection Safeguards which will replace the Deprivation of Liberty Safeguards (DoLS) which were introduced to the MCA in 2007. While DoLS applied only to hospitals and carehomes, the Deprivation of Liberty Safeguards will apply to people in supported accommodation and in their own homes. These are part of the act and will like the DoLs include a functional test of capacity; a person must be able to:

- understand information given about a decision
- retain the information and appreciate its relevance
- use the information to make a decision
- communicate a choice

In Marcus' case I do not believe that he was able to understand the reality of the situation and the consequences of his actions. I do believe that he would have been able to communicate his choice, but that this choice was one motivated only by his irrepressible urge to drink and as such was not a reasoned choice.

A very similar case to Marcus' one is the case of Tower Hamlets v PB (2020) EWCOP34 and I expect there are many more. In this case PB had a long-term history of alcohol abuse. He was in court to assess his mental capacity. The consultant psychiatrist confirmed that PB understood the need to drink in moderation. However, he later changed his mind based upon the fact that the man did not understand that he was unable to control his drinking habits. The judge ruled that purely because PB chose to make unwise decisions was not enough reason to decide that he lacked capacity.

The judge said that the focus should be on the person's capacity to make a decision, not on the possible outcome. People are allowed to make unwise decisions.

The judge understood that PB overestimated his ability to control his drinking but that this still didn't render him incapacitated. Being in denial of a condition as many alcoholics are, would not mean that he did not have mental capacity; he was able to articulate and reason his argument. If he was able to understand that the consequences might be that he would be homeless and even that he might die then it was his decision to make. (He understood the relevant information). The judge said that the court was obligated to protect the autonomy of the individual, not their wellbeing or best interests.

I would question the concept of denial and suggest that denial could be as a result of confusion of mixed up memories, such that an individual believes what he says to be true, despite any evidence to the contrary. Therefore, I would propose that he was maybe not truly able to understand the information presented to him, such that he could use it to make a decision.

The judge in a court of protection is to make a decision on a person's mental capacity, not on his ability to resist a drink; hence the decisions made. However, my point is not only that a long-term alcoholic is not able to resist the urge to drink again but that his brain is in such a condition as to render him 'incapacitated'. To my mind, although he seems to be able to hold a conversation and make a reasoned argument; this is not one based on reality and as such is not the mental capacity of a sane mind. Indeed, in 1881 he would have been classed as a dipsomaniac, (as having periodical inebriety, due to psychical degeneration) and committed to an asylum (Mann, 1881).

The fact that a long-term alcoholic's brain is incapacitated due to alcohol consumption is my argument, and in particular a person's ability to make a decision when suffering from ARBD as this part of their brain (in the frontal lobe) has been damaged. A person's ability to make a decision is based on the fact that they understand relevant information presented. I think that a long-term alcoholic would say that he understood, whilst he is actually unable to demonstrate that understanding, by taking appropriate action. To me, that shows that they didn't in fact understand the relevant information.

The MCA states that a person lacks capacity if he is unable to make a decision due to 'an impairment' of the brain. I would argue that in Marcus' case the damage to his brain was sufficient to be classed as an impairment. I am sure that alcoholism is indeed an impairment to the functioning of the brain. It is defined by Elkins, (2020) as a *chronic disease of the* brain'. ARBD attacks the frontal lobe which controls the decision-making processes and many other major thought processes; these will be discussed further in the following chapter.

A further consideration is that although a person has a right to make poor or unwise decisions, where a person is lacking in mental capacity such that they are making decisions which are seriously detrimental to their health and possibly life-threatening in such cases then maybe a reassessment would be sagacious.

Surely there should be an understanding that alcoholism is something that extirpates the ability to make the wise decision to stop drinking. An alcoholic at the stage that Marcus was at (and possibly PB too) is obviously not going to be able to simply regulate his drinking habits. To assume that he will do so purely because he says that he will seems ludicrous, given the overwhelming evidence to the contrary. He is not in reality able to understand or rationalise the consequences of what he is saying. To me, they are empty words and reflect only the state of his confounded brain.

In the 19th century, Mann, 1881 (MD) understood that addiction to alcohol was a degenerative disease of the brain. He distinguished between a man who can choose to indulge in liquor to excess and the one whose craving is so strong as to overpower even his own desire to defy the urge to drink.

He detailed how such a person is aware that drinking will lead to the state of drunkenness and its subsequent negative consequences and that he may even *'contemplate it with horror and disgust'* (this may be the reason for denial – my thoughts), but,

> *"by an irresistible impulse, he is impelled to gratify his morbid propensity, during the paroxysm, blind to the higher emotions and pursuing a course against which reason and conscience rebel."* (Mann, 1881 p361)

In the 21st century it seems, that we still do not understand this condition as well as this doctor in 1881, that is, that alcoholism causes an impairment of the brain, which the sufferer is unable to counter.

More recent research which accords with that of Mann, is from Nakamura-Palacious (2013) who avers that if the frontal lobe is damaged, as is likely by heavy alcohol consumption, then an alcoholic may know that his behaviour will lead to disastrous consequences, but he is unable to control the behaviour that will lead him there. As such, the ability of his brain to have 'normal capacity' is seriously impaired. Executive function and general mental status are affected differently by the long-term use of alcohol. A long-term alcoholic may lose ability to inhibit inadequate or injurious behaviours.

In as much as the judges are acting in accordance with the law and according to the information put before them, of what may appear to be a reasoned person, they are not considering that the brain may in fact be so impaired as to obfuscate the person's mental abilities, so that what they are really seeing is just a facade. I feel that, in Marcus' case, they were hoodwinked by his eloquence.

Chapter 9

The Effect of Alcohol on the Brain

An investigation of the effects of alcohol on the brain can assist further understanding of the alcoholic condition.

A small amount of alcohol can have positive effects on the body and the mind. Consuming small quantities of alcohol can reduce the risk of heart disease and possibly diabetes. Alcohol causes the release of chemicals to the brain such as dopamine and serotonin which positively affect mood. Dopamine for example, makes a person feel happy and motivated, and can also have a sedative effect and help to induce sleep. However, as more alcohol is consumed the dopamine and serotonin levels drop, inducing a state of depression rather than a high, and restlessness, rather than sleep.

As is easily observable, after the initial 'feelgood' period of alcohol consumption, if a person continues to drink more than the liver is able to process, toxins begin to enter the brain via the blood and cause the body to begin to suffer from the slurring of speech and vision, impairment of memory, slow reaction times and difficulty with movement and judgement. This is because the alcohol affects the frontal lobe in the brain which regulates emotions and mood; personality; evaluation of rewards; impulses; social behaviours; attention, focus and concentration; working memory; reasoning and judgement; organisation, planning and sequencing; speech and language and voluntary movement. It is easy to understand how the drinker may start to have reactions, thoughts and behaviours that they would not have when sober.

When the frontal lobe suffers from alcohol toxicity there are mainly problems with attention and working memory. The damage caused has also been linked with the inability to abstain from alcohol as the individual may have difficulty solving problems, concentrating and be unable to make decisions for the future; they may become inflexible in their ability to change decisions. It may also adversely affect the cells in the parietal lobe leaving the person unable to work out spatial problems such as puzzles; reasoning is affected.

After a period of abstention, for a person who drinks infrequently or small amounts, the brain usually recovers, and the drinker returns to their normal state. There are also factors which affect the extent to which alcohol may affect the brain such as:

- The age a person started drinking and how long they have been drinking
- How much and how often a person drinks
- The person's age, gender, education, genetic background and family history of alcoholism
- General health status (Cox et al., 2004)

In Marcus' case, he had been drinking for a very long time (40-50 years). He had been drinking heavily and often (daily). There was maybe a genetic disposition to alcohol dependence. There is a possible disposition to alcohol dependence just because he is male. Men display a higher prevalence for alcoholism (Ceylan-Isik et al., 2010). He is, at the time of writing, seventy years of age, he is well educated. Other than education and general health status (he has been a very physically fit man); these factors would all impact negatively upon his propensity to become alcoholic. I believe that Marcus' exercise regimen and food consumption have played a crucial role in Marcus' ability to withstand the deleterious effects of his alcohol consumption.

If the Mental Capacity Act were to be applied when a person was drunk, then they would have an impairment of the brain at that time and would lack capacity at that time to make a decision for themselves. However, of course, being drunk cannot be an excuse for misbehaviour where the person is choosing to drink themselves into this condition of incapacity. When the effects of the alcohol wear off then the person will be capacitated again. However, where the brain has suffered extensive damage, which is permanent, I do not believe that the person can be recapacitated to the point at which they are able to resist further imbibement of alcohol. The effects which lead to incapacity do not wear off.

As the body gets used to alcohol it becomes more tolerant of it and more alcohol needs to be consumed before any effects are noticed. This starts a cycle of increased consumption and can eventually lead to dependency. The effects of long-term damage to the brain through alcohol consumption are very severe.

Long term heavy drinking blocks the absorption of the essential vitamin thiamine (vitamin B1). Thiamine is a vital micronutrient which breaks down carbohydrates into sugar. It is not made by the body but is obtained through a normal healthy diet. It is found in foods such as cereals, pork, fish, legumes and yoghurt. When thiamine is not absorbed, the consequences are loss of weight and appetite, confusion, memory loss, muscle weakness and heart problems. It can also cause tingling and numbness in the feet and hands. The only consequences in this list which affect brain impairment are 'confusion' and 'memory loss' but a person who is confused and suffering from loss of memory is incapable of making an informed decision. A person who is alcoholic through long term heavy drinking would therefore have a serious brain impairment.

In the case of Marcus however, whilst he had been in hospital in 2019, I suspect that he had been given thiamine supplements and had recovered from the most serious of the physical effects, maybe the mental effects of thiamine deficiency were also ameliorated by this time and his brain was able to make some degree of recovery.

There is sufficient research for us to know that heavy drinking can cause damage to the brain. Sustained alcohol abuse results in the wasting away of brain cells which are responsible for memory, decision making, behaviour and executive functioning. In effect, it reduces mental capacity. It is possible that Marcus was diagnosed with the condition identified as Alcohol Related Brain Damage (ARBD) whilst he was in hospital and a type of this called Alcohol-related Dementia, which could explain why he was put into a care home for dementia patients. As an ex-wife, I am not privy to these details and nor was I particularly interested. I was grateful and relieved that he was there, being well cared for and by all accounts making excellent progress both physically and mentally. Despite this, he was still an alcoholic and at any opportunity would have gone in search of alcohol. This is indeed what happened when he was assessed as having the mental capacity to make his own decision on where to live and subsequently have access to alcohol.

Alcohol-related Dementia is a type of ARBD which affects the frontal lobe and causes it to shrink. Heavy alcohol consumption exaggerates the shrinkage commensurate with age (Kubota et al., 2001). It is caused by excessive and prolonged alcohol consumption. Symptoms include memory loss, confusion, inability to have empathy with others, difficulty with focus, reasoning, planning and organisation, loss of motivation and difficulty with decision-making and self-monitoring. It may also effect personality changes and lack of balance. With these symptoms it would seem impossible to make the decision to deny the craving to consume alcohol. Damage to the frontal lobe may render people suggestible, such that they will respond to questions with suggested answers, trying to give the 'right' or expected answers.

According to medical organisations such as the American Psychiatric Association, the American Society of Addiction Medicine, The National Center on Addiction and Substance Abuse, The National Institute on Drug Abuse and The National Institute on Alcohol Abuse and Alcoholism, alcohol addiction is a disease. If this is the case, then Marcus will never actually have a real choice of whether or not to take the next drink unless he is cured of the disease. He will always make the unwise choice; so, is he actually making the choice? I would argue that he is not.

Please read this again:

> *[for a long-term alcoholic] "abstaining from alcohol is **nearly impossible** without medical treatment."* (Elkins, 2020)

Clearly this must infer that an individual who is suffering from severe alcoholism to the extent that Marcus is, is unable to make the choice to stop drinking. Why then are social and medical services telling me that it is his choice to drink and a judge deciding that legally he has a right to this choice when to make this decision is *'nearly impossible'* due to suffering from ARBD?

It seems that recovery from alcohol addiction is possible when the individual is at the early stages. With even a few days of detoxification and withdrawal from consumption the shrinkage of the brain causing, memory loss, concentration deficit and increased impulsivity can recover. In other parts of the brain the death of brain cells is irreversible. Recovery varies in different regions of the brain (van Eijk et al., 2012). Further research from van Eijk et al., shows that even a 2-week abstinence from alcohol can result in an improvement in brain function in alcoholics. However, this research refers to a 3-day withdrawal period. Marcus was in hospital for a considerably longer period. It would seem logical that the longer a person has been alcoholic then the greater is the damage to the brain and the longer a recovery period might take. Ende, in this research is quoted,

> *"The ultimate goal of alcoholism treatment is the maintenance of abstinence."*

This is supposing that this is possible for the patient. She goes on to say,

> "To achieve this, the affected person needs to suppress their drinking urges and relearn to value other pleasures. Brain volume hinders this difficult process."

Zahr adds,

> "A minimal of brain healing may be necessary before the addict is able to achieve the control necessary to maintain continued abstinence."

There is a minimum set of cognitive abilities necessary to conquer drug addiction. If the parts of the brain necessary for these abilities to function are already destroyed, then recovery is no longer possible; the extent of brain impairment may be such that a long-term alcoholic may not be able to make the choice to abstain. It is possible that he may agree to commit to abstinence when asked, however his brain may be such that he is not actually making that decision, merely looking like he is making that decision.

The cognitive impairments which result from alcoholism are the parts of the brain which need to be engaged to initiate and maintain the behavioural changes necessary for recovery. This vicious cycle no doubt contributes to relapse.

It is possible that the parts of his brain which would allow Marcus to actually make a reasoned decision are no longer available to him. His brain is not informing him correctly. He is able to speak, but, as is seen later, the words he is speaking eventually become more and more nonsensical. Even, recalling the Oman scenario, twenty years ago, he was not able to reason that it would be exceedingly unlikely that anyone would bug the office of a librarian. To imagine that he could now undertake future planning such that he could also reason and plan how he could combat his alcohol addiction seems ridiculous, with the knowledge we now have of brain deterioration and damage due to excessive and continued alcohol consumption.

In the case of Tower Hamlets v PB, the psychiatrist confirmed that PB understood the need to drink in moderation, presumably this is because he said he did. However, it is possible that the man was in a suggestive state due to brain damage and would endeavour to give the 'right' answers.

I spoke with Marcus in hospital in 2019 and told him that if he drank again, it could possibly kill him. I asked him if he understood this and the consequences of drinking again. He told me that he did. Of course, he either did not understand it or was in a suggestive state and as maybe also PB in the Tower Hamlets case and was merely seeking to give me the 'right' answer. At this moment, three years later, he is back in hospital having been evicted from his accommodation due to alcohol abuse.

A further and very serious consequence of long-term brain damage due to alcoholism which Marcus is possibly now suffering from is Wernicke-Korsakoff Syndrome (US Department of Health and Human Services, 2004). There are two stages:

Stage 1 Wernicke's encephalopathy which causes spasms, confusion and paralysis of the eye muscles. This is curable with the administering of thiamine. Up to 80%

of alcoholics have a deficiency in thiamine. This can progress to:

Stage 2 Korsakoff psychosis. This results in permanent memory loss and confabulation (creation of new but untrue memories), learning problems, hallucinations, unsteadiness and dementia. This is incurable.

This could well be the alcohol-induced psychosis that the nurse in the hospital where Marcus now resides alluded to. Why have they waited until the condition is 'uncurable'?

According to a report RCP CR185, (2014) Wernicke-Korsakoff Syndrome is an extreme type of ARBD. In its mildest form are frontal lobe dysfunctions. They state that 75% of people with ARBD improve with appropriate care. ARBD is described by them as *a silent problem* with information from post-mortems showing that,

> *"0.5-1.5% of the general adult population have changes in their brain as a consequence of alcohol misuse and most of these do not have a diagnosis recorded in clinical case notes during their lifetime." (Cook et al., 1998 in CR185)*

They subsequently reported that according to Wilson et al., (2012), that,

> *"with appropriate care – relapse into alcohol misuse runs at 10% and there is a 10% mortality rate."*

They believe that appropriate services which provide a rehabilitative model could reduce all acute hospital day-bed usage by 85%. There is evidence that the alcoholic brain **can** make recovery, but only through the taking of drugs and therapy and that it has most chance of success when the alcohol abuse is in its early stages. Later stages may also be treated.

The appropriate care suggested for severe alcohol-related brain damage follows a five-stage psychosocial and cognitive rehabilitation model:

Stage 1 – stabilisation and withdrawal

Stage 2 – protected, calm and stable environment, abstinence from alcohol, good nutrition, mood stabilisation, regularisation of sleep pattern, calm and psychosocial support, engagement of specialist treatment services, family involvement, memory and orientation cues and structured hygiene routines. (2-3 months)

Stage 3 – psychosocial rehabilitation, cognitive-behaviour treatment for depression if required, continuing assessment and monitoring. (Up to 3 years)

Stage 4 – establishment in an environment which encourages as much independence as possible.

Stage 5 – structural activities and daily routines to promote long term independence and minimise the likelihood of relapse.

Facilities which provide such care need to be set up. Marcus has not had this care.

In the case of Wernicke-Korsakoff Syndrome, its poor prognosis if left untreated is historically a 20% fatality rate (Harper et al., 1986). The longer the person continues to drink, the greater the damage done to the brain and the longer recovery takes. The more severe the case, the less the likelihood of recovery. The CR185 report also points out that older people are less likely to recover cognitive function than younger people. This report further recommends that services are commissioned to care for local population needs. The research and recommendations are out there but in the case of Marcus I feel that the services have failed him.

Another permanent problem which can arise is hepatic encephalopathy where the liver can no longer filter toxins such as manganese and ammonia from the blood. These toxins then circulate through the body to the brain and damage the brain tissue. This can result in the brain slowing down, it may eventually shut down and leave the person in a coma.

In a situation where a person drinks much more alcohol than their body can tolerate; they may suffer from an alcoholic overdose. This can cause the areas of the brain which control life supporting functions to shut down – breathing, heart-rate and temperature. It can cause permanent brain damage and death. I know of one occurrence of this where a friend's husband who did not generally drink at all, went out with friends and had too many drinks. He died in his bathroom when he got home as he had a very low tolerance to alcohol due to hardly drinking.

Although regular drinking builds tolerance it simultaneously has a cumulative damaging effect on the brain.

I am pondering now, the point to continue writing. I feel the situation for Marcus is quite hopeless. I only hope that in the future, someone else will address the problems sooner, knowing that this is where it will lead.

Anyhow, I'll return to the subject of the MCA and the second point which refers to *'material time'*. When is the material time at which the person needs to take a decision?

The Mental Capacity Act (2005) Code of Practice (2007) explains this as:

> *"at the time the decision or action needs to be taken."*

In the case of Marcus, I would argue that he is unable to decide to not imbibe an alcoholic drink at the time when he needs to take that decision. There is repeated evidence of this being the case. He is unable to understand or be aware of the consequences of this action such that he abstains. The continued and persistent repetition of taking alcohol for over forty years has resulted in impairment of his brain such that he is unable to make the decision to abstain and act upon it. If the time refers to his decision to want to change accommodation, then of course, he can communicate his wish to do this at the appropriate time. As the ultimate goal for him is to get another drink, as previously propounded, he has only one recourse and that is to be free to satisfy his craving.

If a person is inebriated, it is reasonable to suggest that they are incapacitated. Would a person be expected to make an important decision when they were drunk? Certainly not. In the case of ARBD the effect upon the frontal lobe of the brain is that the brain is in this permanent state of incapacity. It also inhibits the person from making a reasonably informed decision as memory and decision-making are impaired. As mentioned previously, with ARBD it can be almost impossible for a person to make the decision not to drink. If a person's brain is permanently in this condition, how can he possibly have mental capacity at any time? In my opinion (that only of a layperson) he has the mental capacity of a baby wanting to keep his dummy.

Chapter 10

Discussion

In our society we have the right to make our own decisions about our lives. A person without a brain impairment knows that there is risk involved in drinking alcohol, there is risk of loss of control of mental and physical faculties; there is also the long-term risk of addiction where consumption is of high quantities and prolonged duration. There are risks to most activities, sports, driving or even crossing a road, but we are generally able to assess these risks and take appropriate action to keep ourselves physically safe. A problem with alcohol consumption is that it affects our mental state; this is more difficult to self-assess. Whilst we can see physical deterioration or damage, we cannot necessarily see mental deterioration or damage. Maybe we are also unable to detect changes in our own mental state due to the changes themselves.

Most people who enjoy having a drink, do so for recreational purposes, for relaxing at the end of the day, to maybe suppress any anxieties, or to help them to sleep, to enjoy watching their friends lose inhibitions and balance, such that they become amusing and/or being part of the same activities or simply as part of an accepted socio-cultural practice of being out with a group of friends. Many people are in this category and do not become alcoholic.

People have the right to make decisions which affect their own life. The law (The Mental Capacity Act, 2005) states that a person cannot be treated as lacking capacity to make a decision because they make an unwise one. This is the reason that Marcus was able to go to court and claim that he was being deprived of his liberty, by being detained in a care home. He is an articulate individual and was able to argue that he understood that drinking alcohol was destructive and possibly even said that he would moderate his drinking habits. The real issue however, was that he was not able to say that he was unable to moderate his drinking habits which was in fact the case. This major point was overlooked.

I was very much aggrieved that the lady at social services seemed to regard Marcus as being undeserving; although it is an opinion that I am sure, is echoed by many. The doctor also believed that he brought this state on himself. How can a man who deliberately brought this on himself be deserving of any sympathy or have any time and services wasted on him? The myth that he is choosing to drink needs to be dispelled. I now know that this opinion is only one of ignorance, but question how society in general and the professionals in particular, are not aware of information which was in fact available in 1881?

The sad reality is that whilst a man is a little drunk and entertaining, and he is the life and soul of the party, he is a great guy. But once he's addicted to this lifestyle and unable to escape from it and becomes drunk and in the gutter, he is regarded as trash to be pitied – 'shame, he couldn't hold his drink'. There is no help and little chance of recovery. How does society in the 21st Century hold this view? It seems archaic. Why didn't he seek help? As you may now appreciate, the answer is, because he was physically and mentally unable to resist or combat his completely uncontrollable impulse to drink. This is the same reason why he would fervently rebut suggestions that he was alcoholic and spurn any attempts to help him and why he would never acquiesce to anything that may force him to relinquish alcohol; it had a firm and deadly grip on him from which there was little chance of escape. Even after a long time of abstention the alcoholic may be lured back to the abyss from whence he came. Marcus has only survived up to now, I believe due to the exercise and good nutrition he enjoyed in his younger days.

At what point will any services rescue him? The answer seems clear; when he himself asks for help. For this to happen he would have to have the mental capacity to do so, which he does not. I have been told by social services and his doctor that it is his choice to drink. Unless this perception changes and the ignorance of the truth of the matter, then the inevitable consequences will continue to befall those who submit to the lure of a substance which enhances their appreciation of life and then snares them into a life of slavery to it.

Marcus is unable to choose not to drink. He is also now unaware of his own inability. He is compelled to consume to the point of complete incapacity, where he loses control of his bodily functions. He has also now lost his mind to the point of hallucination and delusion. This condition is daily and persistent. He is denied accommodation because of his condition, resulting in the inevitable situation of homelessness.

There is no glory now. No *'he's a jolly good fellow'* anymore. His wife has left him, his working years are well behind him, his friends have deserted him. His children live far away and can only offer support over the phone. His life is lonely and one of isolation. There is only the reward of the amber nectar or mother's ruin to provide balm to his predicament, respite from yearning and the dulling of painful senses and recollections. All that seems left is the humiliation of an old man.

Maybe it's true, he brought it on himself. He's an intelligent man, well educated, well brought up, quite capable of seeing what are and what are not sensible choices. But this has been a gradual decline over forty or fifty years which has clearly taken its toll on his brain and body and subsequent mental and physical wellbeing.

The fact is that he does have a right to make his own choices, but my argument is that he doesn't in fact have the mental capacity to do so. What he does have is an intelligent brain, lengthy experience in the practice of deception and the ability to construct and articulately present his arguments almost with recurring automaticity. The problem is that his arguments are not based upon rational thought and an ability to comprehend the outcome of his decisions. This is not due to lack of intelligence but due to damage caused to his brain. This unfortunate state of damage he has indeed brought about himself. But should this be held against him when he can no longer, because of this incapacity, effect a rational choice?

For many years I would have described Marcus as a 'high-functioning alcoholic'. He was able to go to work and perform effectively, behave reasonably, perform well at interviews to get new jobs, book and go on holidays and conduct what looked from the outside to be a normal family life.

Some of the indicators in Marcus' case, that he was in fact a high functioning alcoholic, included the fact that he would vehemently refute any suggestion that he might be drinking too much and would refuse to enter conversation about it. He would conceal his actual consumption by saying that he drank less than he did and he always appeared well groomed and dressed. He was always able to conduct an intelligent conversation and certainly did so when it came to rationalising his drinking habits. He always said that it was normal, that everyone drank and that it did not cause him any problems. To some extent, this was true.

There were, however, red flags, more so when we were married than when we were dating, as we spent more time together. He was not able to perform any tasks after teatime, but he did usually shop for and prepare the evening meals and we certainly ate well. He could not ignore his craving for alcoholic beverages for any one day or in the evenings perform any tasks requiring mental exertion; he could certainly not drive of course, and usually spent his evenings watching TV accompanied by a selection of alcoholic drinks.

Could I or should I have done more to help him? I did try, but as said previously, any suggestion that he should speak to a professional about this habit was met with verbal aggression and to insist further would only have resulted in a pointless argument.

Something needs to change to help those in Marcus' predicament and their loved ones. I propose the following arguments and recommendations:

1   Marcus (in my opinion) did not have mental capacity as defined by the Mental Health Act,

2005 because, he was not able to understand the consequences of the information he was being given – this was in fact an erroneous decision.

In 1881 his state would have been classed as having *'periodical insanity'* (Mann, 1881), yet in 2019 he was classed as having 'mental capacity'.

2   Marcus' brain was sufficiently damaged to completely inhibit any attempt to resist the urge to drink alcohol – he was not and is not *'choosing to drink'*.

In 1881 Marcus would have been diagnosed as dipsomanic and as such been regarded as suffering from an *'irresistible impulse impelling him to gratify his morbid propensity'* (Mann, 1881). It was recognised even so long ago, that such a sufferer is actually incapable of resisting the urge to drink.

3   If Marcus had not been allowed to leave the care home he was admitted to, then he would have not developed psychosis due to continued alcohol consumption

Mann described the chronic state as *'the most incurable'* of the disease and suggested that only seclusion in an asylum with total abstention from alcohol could possibly effect a cure, as *'a discharge is always followed with a repetition of the same acts'*. We knew this in 1881. There is no safety net now or protection for this elderly and deluded man. He was three years ago, thrown back into the jaws of the lion named 'Alcohol' with no hope of forestalling his fate.

4   Rehabilitation facilities need to be available for long-term alcoholics and also for those who may be prevented from further decline.

There are reports calling for such action - Cox et al., (2004) and RCP CR185, (2014), for example. No action seems to be forthcoming.

If the chronic disease of alcoholism requires ongoing medical attention, then I would suggest that any treatment should be administered to the point at which those responsible for caring for the patient are quite sure that the individual is able to resist the craving before they are allowed the freedom to make that choice again. In Marcus' case he was allowed to leave the secure facility before this point.

5   It should not be assumed that because a person appears to be able to construct a persuasive argument, that they are able to do so based on mental capacity. Tests of mental capacity should be more rigorous.

6   There is a failure in the law to understand the nature of alcoholism and its deleterious effect on the brain. This was true in 1881 as the statement below shows:

> *"Our laws, at present, fail lamentably in preventing intemperance*, and this is due, in a great measure, to the false view in which the disease, is held by the judiciary."* (Mann, 1881)

*Intemperance means lack of moderation or restraint

7   Further research should be funded into the impact of alcohol on the brain and how

deterioration can be identified and maybe prevented earlier.

8   The provision of social education to change the perspective of alcoholism as a choice, should be provided and information to help people to identify those who might need help, with guidance on what to do.

9   Lower alcohol content in alcoholic beverages could help to reduce the excesses of alcohol consumption.

10   Education about the risks and limits of 'safe' alcohol consumption should be provided in schools, colleges and workplaces.

The laws, our systems and our services are still failing with regard to dealing with the problem of alcoholism. In the 21st century we should have an increased awareness of the psychical degeneration of the brain due to alcohol intake and should be taking preventative measures to help people suffering from this condition. It should no longer be acceptable to consider that a person is 'choosing to drink', once they are in fact not able to make the decision not to.

As I conclude this book, I hope that it will provide impetus for some change in the way that alcoholism is perceived, and that legislation can change to reflect the growing research which shows that a long-term alcoholic does not have mental capacity if he is suffering from the Wernicke-Korsakoff type of ARBD and most certainly Korsakoff's Psychosis.

As I write the final pages, Marcus is in hospital relating stories he believes to be real but are actually fit for a TV series, of police stings, police corruption, people being shot, strings of arrests, the finding of millions of pounds under hidden hatches, dead bodies in swimming pools and his sons solving crimes as police inspectors.

With the suggestion that he is suffering from alcohol-induced psychosis. I can only hope against hope, that this is a sufficient diagnosis to finally get him the help he so desperately needs. How far does a person have to fall before it's too late? I would imagine that it is too late to save or recover his brain function; thankfully and unbelievably he seems to be physically in a reasonably good state of health and certainly better than when he was found three years ago on the park bench. However, he does seem to definitely be non compos mentis.

My friend's observation showed that he is conflating reality with fiction. However, he believes his stories to be true; to him they are factual. Some true recollections from long ago surface and are accurate. He can appear lucid and present the façade that all is well in his mind. But, his brain function is seriously depleted; he is no more able to resist the uncontrollable impulse to take alcoholic stimulants which cause intoxication, than he is to pilot a rocket.

Marcus' ability to engage reasoning and judgement, impulse control, problem solving and decision making are severely diminished. He cannot reason what is real or not and certainly not reason and take action on a decision in the future. When people challenge his perceptions and beliefs he cannot understand why and sees this as them deliberately trying to find fault or upset him. He is permanently confused.

As if that is not enough, he is overwhelmed by a craving for alcohol, and to seek out the environments, people and experiences which he has learned (and is not able to unlearn) to associate with alcohol and of which alcohol enhances his enjoyment. These are not deliberate or conscious acts but the result of his brain malfunctioning. All these factors conspire against him. His mixed up thoughts are his reality. Marcus' brain is causing him to believe what he is saying now, in the same way that it led him to earnestly defend his conviction that he was not addicted to alcohol. He has no control over this.

Whilst family, friends and observers are getting annoyed at the apparent lies being spun, despite, maybe an outward façade of capacity, due to the ability of the sufferer to speak intelligibly; the alcoholic's seriously damaged brain is unable to retain information or to distinguish fact from fiction; his short-term memories are jumbled. Add to this, hallucinations and delusions and his life must be akin to something in a horror movie. It seems to me that the real horror is that society believes in an illusory truth and proclaims that Marcus and those like him, *'choose to drink'*, when there is overwhelming evidence that the real truth is that this choice is in fact **Hobson's Choice**.

References

The Bill of Rights Bill. (not yet enacted) [Accessed online on 6.11.22] at: www.ukandeu.ac.uk

Boness, C. L., Lane, S. P., Sher K. J. (2019) Not All Alcohol Use Disorder Criteria Are Equally Severe: Toward Severity Grading of Individual Criterial in College Drinkers. Psychology of Addictive Behaviours.

Buddy, T. (2020) The Link Between Early Drinking Age and Risk of Alcoholism. VeryWellMind. [Accessed online on 7.11.22] at: www.verywellmind.com

Ceylan-Isik, A. F., McBride, S. M. and Ren, J. (2010) Sex Difference in Alcoholism: Who is at a greater risk for Development of Alcoholic Complication? [Accessed online on 3.11.22] at: www.ncbi.nlm.nih.gov

Cox, S., Anderson, I. and McCabe, L. (2004) A Fuller Life: Report of The Expert Group on Alcohol and Related Brain Damage. Dementia Services Development Centre. University of Stirling. Scottish Executive.

Deprivation of liberty Safeguards - 2020-21. [Accessed online on 6.11.22] at: www.gov.uk

Edenberg, H. J. and Foroud, T. (2013) Nature reviews. Gastroenterology & hepatology. 10(8): 487-494.

van Eijk, J, Demirakca, T., Frischknecht, U., Hermann, D., Mann, K. and Ende, G. (2012) Rapid Partial Regeneration of Brain Volume During the first 14 Days of Abstinence from Alcohol. Alcoholism: Clinical and

Experimental Research. [Accessed online on 28.10.22] at: www.sciencedaily.com

Elkins, C. (2020) Is Alcoholism a Disease or a Choice? [Accessed online on 7.11.22] at: www.drugrehab.com

Gmel, G., Marmet, S., Studer, J. and Wicki, M. (2020) Are changes in Personality Traits and Alcohol Use Associated? A Cohort Study Among Young Swiss Men. Frontiers.

Harper, C., Giles, M., & Finlay-Jones, R. (1986). Clinical signs in the Wernicke-Korsakoff complex: A retrospective analysis of 131 cases diagnosed at necropsy. Journal of Neurology, Neurosurgery & Psychiatry. 49(4): 341-345.

IAS. (undated) Institute of Alcohol Studies. A brief history of the UK's low risk drinking guidelines. [Accessed online on 30.10.22] at: www.ias.org.uk

Kendler, K. S., Gardner, C., D and Dick, D. M. (2011) Predicting alcohol consumption in adolescence from alcohol-specific and general externalizing genetic risk factors, key environmental exposures and their interaction. Psychol. Med. 41. 1505-1516.

Kubota, M., Nakazaki, S, Hirai, S., Saeki, N., Yamaura, A., and Kusaka, T. (2001) Alcohol consumption and frontal lobe shrinkage: study of 1432 non-alcoholic subjects. Journal of Neurology, Neurosurgery and Psychiatry. 71(1).

Mann, E. C. (1881) The Nature, Pathology and Treatment of Dipsomania. The Southern Medical Record. New York. [Accessed online on 4.11.22] at: www.europepmc.org

Matrix News. (2020) One in five children will drink alcohol this Christmas. [Accessed online on 7.11.22] at: www.matrixdiagnostics.co.uk

Mental Capacity Act 2005 Code of Practice. (2007) TSO, Crown Copyright. London.

Mental Health Act 1984 Code of Practice. (2015) TSO, Crown Copyright. London. [Accessed online on 6.11.22] at: www.gov.uk

MESAS. (2020) Monitoring and Evaluating Scotland's Alcohol Strategy. Monitoring Report Public Health Scotland. [Accessed on 29.10.22] at: www.publichealthscotland.scot

Morikawa, H. and Harris, R. A. (2011) Small K channels: Big targets for treating alcoholism? Biological Psychiatry. 69(7): 614-615.

Nakamura-Palacios, E. M., Souza, R. S. M., Zago-Gomes, M. P, de Melo, A. M. F., Braga, F. S, Kubo, T. T. A., and Gasparetto, E. L. (2013) Gray Matter Volume in Left Rostal Middle Frontal and Left Cerebellar Cortices Predicts Frontal Executive Performance in alcoholic Subjects. Alcoholism: Clinical and Experimental Research. [Accessed online on 2.11.22] at www.sciencedaily.com

National Institute on Drug Abuse. (2019) Genetics and epigenetics of addiction. DrugFacts. [Accessed online on 1.11.22] at: www.nida.nih.gov

National Institute on Alcohol Abuse and Alcoholism. (NIAAA[1]) The Healthcare Professional's. Core Resource on Alcohol. Risk Factors: Varied Vulnerability to Alcohol-Related Harm. [Accessed online on 1.11.22] at: www.niaaa.nih.gov

National Institute on Alcohol Abuse and Alcoholism. (NIAAA[2]) Alcohol Use Disorder: A Comparison Between DSM-IV and DSM-5. [Accessed online on 1.11.22] at: www.niaaa.nih.gov

National Institute on Alcohol Abuse and Alcoholism. (NIAAA[3]) Alcohol and the Brain: An Overview. [Accessed online on 1.11.22] at: www.niaaa.nih.gov

National Records of Scotland. (2022) Alcohol-specific Deaths 2021 Report. [Accessed online on 6.11.22] at: nsscotland.gov.uk

RCP CR185. (2014) Alcohol and Brain Damage in Adults With reference to high-risk groups. The Royal College of Psychiatrists. College Report CR185.

Scottish Health Survey. (2019) Volume 1: Main Report. Chapter 4: Alcohol. [Accessed online on 6.11.22] at: www.gov.scot

The secret history of Special Brew. (2015) [accessed online on 31.10.22] at: www.bbc.com

Slaughter, E., Sharp, A. and Fuller, K. (2022) Genetics and Addiction: Is Alcoholism Hereditary or Genetic? American Addiction Centers. [Accessed online on 20.10.22] at: www.americanaddictioncenters.org

Stewart, C. (2021) Alcohol Use in the UK Statistics & Facts [Accessed online on 29.10.22] at: www.statista.com

UN-CRPD. (2006) Convention on the Rights of Persons with Disabilities, United Nations. Department of Economic and Social Affairs. Disability. [Accessed online on 6.11.22] at: www.un.org

US Department of Health and Human Services. (2004) Alcohol's Damaging Effects on the Brain. Alcohol Alert. 63.

Wied, S. T., Knebel, M., Tesky, V. A. and Haberstroh, J. (2019) The Human Right to Make One's Own Choices – Implications for Supported Decision-Making in Persons With Dementia: A Systematic Review. European Psychologist. 24 (2): 146-158.

Yang, P., Tao, R., He, C., Liu, S., Wang, Y. and Zhang, X. (2018) The Risk Factors of the Alcohol Use Disorders – Through Review of Its Comorbidities. Frontiers in Neuroscience. 12: 303.

YouGov Survey: Society. (2022) Part Six: Alcohol Consumption. [Accessed online on 7.11.22] at: www.yougov.co.uk

Printed in Great Britain
by Amazon

18899047R00071